Praise for *Wellbeing Rituals*

"*Wellbeing Rituals* provides a practical, holistic roadmap for wellness. Koya Webb covers important areas that many self-help books overlook, including spirituality and nutrition. You are sure to find some inspiring insights in this encompassing and empowering book."

—Thema Bryant,
Pepperdine University professor and author of Matters of the Heart

"Koya Webb is the real deal and *Wellbeing Rituals* is the kind of book that changes your life the way change really happens: one small decision at a time. Success doesn't have to cost you your peace. Let Koya show you how."

—Mel Robbins,
New York Times *bestselling author of* The Let Them Theory*, and host of* The Mel Robbins *podcast*

"Koya's work emphasizes that true wellbeing is built through consistent, intentional action. This book offers readers a structured yet flexible framework for creating balance, clarity, and sustainable vitality."

—Jay Shetty,
number one New York Times *bestselling author and host of the* On Purpose *podcast*

"*Wellbeing Rituals* is a sacred guide for creating daily practices that nourish the body, mind and spirit. Koya offers practical tools to help us live with intention and cultivate harmony in our lives. This book is a powerful companion for anyone seeking balance, clarity and spiritual alignment in a busy world."

—Trent Shelton,
bestselling author and motivational speaker

"I am so proud of Koya, whom I lovingly consider my spiritual daughter. I have seen her navigate life's challenges with grace, resilience, and alignment with the divine. May every reader of *Wellbeing Rituals* be inspired by her journey and use the wisdom she shares to step fully into optimal health, wholeness and holistic wellbeing."

—Queen Afua,
founder of the Sacred Woman Rites of Passage Program and author of Sacred Woman

"In *Wellbeing Rituals*, Koya pours her heart, her story, and her lived wisdom into every page. As someone proud to call her a friend, I've witnessed the authenticity and intention she brings to everything she does, and this book is no exception."

—Taj George,
lead singer of SWV, Grammy-Nominated R&B group

"Empowering, soul-filling … in *Wellbeing Rituals*, Koya guides and inspires you to create a life that's whole, grounded and Divinely aligned! A phenomenal book by a phenomenal woman!"

—Jamie Kern Lima,
New York Times *bestselling author of* WORTHY *and host of* The Jamie Kern Lima Show *podcast*

WELLBEING RITUALS

WELLBEING RITUALS

SCIENCE-BACKED PRACTICES FOR SUSTAINABLE HEALING AND LIVING

KOYA WEBB

Foreword by Reverend Michael Bernard Beckwith,
Founder, Agape International Spiritual Center

WILEY

Published by John Wiley & Sons, Inc., Hoboken, New Jersey.

For general information on our other products and services or for technical support, please contact our Customer Care Department within the United States at (800) 762-2974, outside the United States at (317) 572-3993 or fax (317) 572-4002.

Wiley also publishes its books in a variety of electronic formats. Some content that appears in print may not be available in electronic formats. For more information about Wiley products, visit our web site at www.wiley.com.

Library of Congress Cataloging-in-Publication Data is Available:

ISBN: 9781394387229 (cloth)
ISBN: 9781394387243 (ePub)
ISBN: 9781394387267 (ePDF)

Cover Design: Jon Boylan
Cover Image: Koya Webb
Author Photo: Ron Hill Studio

SKY10154421_042126

For my mother,
who taught me unconditional love—
not only through her strength,
but through her softness, her humanity,
and her unwavering faith in me.

I carry your ring over my heart,
your wisdom in my spirit,
and your love in every breath I take.

This book is for you—
and for everyone learning that holistic wellbeing
is the greatest gift we can give ourselves,
our families,
and the world.

Wellbeing is not about perfection or the absence of challenges but the presence of alignment and intention in every area of life.

Contents

Foreword

It is a profound honor to introduce Koya Webb's transformative new book, *Wellbeing Rituals: Science-Backed Practices for Sustainable Healing and Living*. In this work, Koya offers a luminous pathway for anyone seeking to reconnect with themselves, cultivate lasting wellbeing, and live fully in alignment with their highest potential. I've had the privilege of witnessing Koya's journey over the years—watching her continually step deeper into full embodiment of the Divine, expanding her capacity to lead, teach, and inspire.

Koya is not only a visionary in the field of holistic wellbeing she is also a living example of what it means to integrate mind, body, and spirit in daily life. Her guidance is grounded in decades of experience as a yoga teacher, longevity specialist, life coach, and spiritual guide, and she has inspired millions worldwide through her books, teachings, and transformative work with individuals and organizations alike. In *Wellbeing Rituals*, she offers over 50 science-backed practices that support emotional healing, physical vitality, spiritual connection, and long-term resilience. Through her CHBT method—connect, heal, build, thrive—Koya provides readers with a clear framework to slow down, realign, and cultivate a life of clarity, purpose, and sustained wellbeing.

What sets Koya apart is her authenticity, depth, and unwavering commitment to living the practices she teaches. I have personally witnessed her navigate life's most challenging moments—including the recent transition of her mother—with grace, resilience, and profound faith. She leaned fully into her own methods, demonstrating how to work through grief, regulate the nervous system, and maintain spiritual connection even in times of deep pain. Observing this process was a testament to her mastery and to the transformative power of the rituals she shares.

Koya's impact extends far beyond her personal journey. She has helped millions embody sustainable wellbeing, build mindful lifestyles, and step into empowered versions of themselves. Through her leadership, she has created inclusive spaces that honor diversity, celebrate self-expression, and champion holistic healing. From guiding global audiences in yoga and breathwork to supporting corporate leaders in cultivating emotional intelligence and resilience, her work embodies a rare combination of wisdom, compassion, and tangible results.

As her spiritual father, I am proud of the woman, teacher, and leader she has become. This book is more than a guide. It is a sacred invitation to step into your own power, release what holds you back, and cultivate a life rooted in clarity, vitality, and purpose. *Wellbeing Rituals* offers readers practical tools, spiritual insight, and inspiration to design daily rhythms that nourish the mind, body, and spirit.

May this work illuminate your path, guide you to live fully, and empower you to honor the highest expression of yourself in every moment.

Peace and Richest Blessings,
Michael Bernard Beckwith
Founder and CEO, Agape International Spiritual Center
Author, *Life Visioning* and *Spiritual Liberation*;
host, *Take Back Your Mind* podcast

Overview

We are living in an age of unprecedented burnout, anxiety, and disconnection. Our lives are saturated with noise: social media, divisive politics, climate grief, and the lingering impacts of a global pandemic. What we are facing is not only a health crisis but also a spiritual crisis, a fracture in our connection to ourselves, each other, nature, and the Divine.

Wellbeing Rituals is both a lifeline and a compass for these times. It is not just another wellness book; it is a sacred space designed to help you connect, heal, build, and thrive. Inside, you will find rituals (simple, sacred, science-backed, and sustainable daily practices) that help you find true joy, meaning, and peace in your life.

At its core, this book is about daily rituals that energetically align your actions with your beliefs and values. Over 20 years of wellness practice, coaching, and spiritual study have gone into creating this guide, which brings together science, personal stories, client stories (with names changed), and soul.

You will explore the seven areas of wellbeing (spiritual, emotional, mental, nutritional, physical, social, and financial) and learn my Connect, Heal, Build, Thrive Method, a cyclical framework for transformation. Together, these create a foundation for complete life alignment.

This is not a book to skim or leave on a shelf. It's a companion, a mirror, a resource you will return to again and again as you create a life that is whole, grounded, and divinely aligned.

My mission is for *Wellbeing Rituals* to be more than a book. My intention is for it to be a movement, one that inspires millions of people to choose alignment over burnout, wholeness over perfection, and ritual over routine.

Welcome to your journey home to yourself.

Prologue

Expect the unexpected.

I never thought this day would come, walking down the aisle to say "I do" at a beautiful all-inclusive resort in Mexico, surrounded by my favorite people. The one thing I found the hardest to manifest was finally coming true. And it was no cakewalk. In the months before, my husband-to-be had gotten into a car accident and injured his back, my bank account was bleeding after a two-year unintended soft girl season, and I was overwhelmed just trying to make this dream a reality.

As I shifted the sand beneath my toes, my mom and dad looked at me with proud smiles. My mom asked to walk down the aisle with us and I said, "Absolutely." We had healed so much in our relationship. She was my biggest cheerleader, always saying, "If anyone can do it, you can, Koya. I love you." We had traveled the world together, her dream fulfilled, and made countless magical memories. Never in a million years would I have guessed this would be one of our last.

Now, I write these words through tears, remembering our final destination together. I wear her wedding ring around my neck with my ankh, breathing each breath in her honor. My mother taught me unconditional love . . . God's love, agape love . . . the greatest gift she could ever give. Her strength and her struggles live in me. Her transition reminded me of one of life's greatest truths: expect the unexpected. And when the unexpected comes, we have the opportunity to return to the only thing that can truly sustain us: our total wellbeing.

Introduction

Tohamina / Freepik

What Is Wellbeing?

As a small-town girl from Humboldt, Tennessee, I've always been a student of life. I learned early that happiness requires equal parts grace and grit. But one month before my 40th birthday, at the height of my career, I found myself sitting in the bathtub with tears streaming down my face.

On the outside, I looked successful: leading a team of 21, running a virtual retreat with 8,000 participants, and securing brand deals with global companies. But inside, I was burnt out, lonely, and quietly unraveling. My two-hour self-care routine couldn't keep me from sneaking vodka into my green juice, scrolling instead of sleeping, and dreaming of an escape.

The murder of George Floyd broke what was left of my delusion. It painfully reopened wounds from my brother's childhood abuse by the police. I had to reach out for help because the performative climate I was asked to be a part of was draining the life out of me. Everything felt wrong and I didn't want to be a part of it. With the guidance of an eye movement desensitization and reprocessing therapist, the power of pranayama, powerful texts like *Sacred Woman* by Queen Afua, and my daily rituals, I began healing.

That healing journey revealed a truth that changed everything: success without holistic wellbeing isn't really success at all, and it's definitely not sustainable.

My Invitation to You

Yes . . . *you*:

- The graduate wrestling with how to build a life, not just a career
- The new mother balancing ambition with presence
- The retiree searching for meaning in a new chapter
- The executive questioning whether the sacrifices are worth it
- The immigrant navigating opportunities while missing home
- The father caught between long hours and time with family
- The empty nester asking, "What now?"
- Insert yourself here

Wherever you are, this book is for you.

The rituals I share are not just self-care checklists. They are about alignment: bringing your actions, your beliefs, and your values into harmony. They are about designing a life that feels grounded and true to your soul.

Your path won't look exactly like mine and it isn't supposed to. But the stories, science, and soul infused into these pages will help you pause, reset, and realign.

This book is my invitation to ask yourself the questions that saved me: "Where are you now? Where do you want to be? And are you well enough to get there?"

Are you truly thriving in every area of your life?

Take my Lifestyle Alignment Quiz to uncover exactly where your wellbeing is flourishing and where it's quietly draining your energy. In just a few minutes, you'll get a personalized score across all seven areas of wellbeing and a clear roadmap for improvement.

Bonus: Download the quiz today and get my 1-Page Life Reset Planner to turn your insights into action immediately.

Claim your free quiz & planner now: https://www.koyawebb.com/quiz.

The CHBT (Connect, Heal, Build, Thrive) Method: Your Roadmap to Holistic Wellbeing

The CHBT Method wasn't always called CHBT. When I first began writing this book, it started as the Heal, Build, Thrive Method. I was focused on practical tools, on steps to repair, strengthen, and rise. And then, something shifted.

One quiet evening, as I poured my soul onto the page, I felt a gentle nudge, a whisper from Spirit. It wasn't an idea I generated; it was a divine download. "Your soul is already whole," the message said. "You don't need to fix it. You need to connect to it."

That moment changed everything. Connect became the first step, not because anything was missing, but because alignment begins with recognition. Your soul doesn't need to be healed; it's always been intact, luminous, and complete, waiting for you to return to it. All it asks is that you show up. That is why CHBT begins with Connect.

These rituals, practices, and daily invitations are not about rushing to the finish line. They are about presence, awareness, and gentle evolution. You don't need to do everything at once. The most powerful shifts happen one day at a time, one breath at a time. Slowly, steadily, you will notice your strength returning—not just physically, but emotionally, mentally, and spiritually. The weight of old patterns lifts. Clarity replaces chaos. Peace replaces resistance.

The pursuit of wellbeing is no longer a lifestyle choice, it's a declaration. A declaration that you are committed to living fully, authentically, and intentionally. In today's fast-paced, overstimulated world, too many of us navigate life on autopilot, disconnected from our inner wisdom, our physical vitality, and the relationships that nourish our soul. The CHBT Method is your invitation to reclaim your energy, your clarity, and your sense of purpose.

This method is more than a set of practices; it is a framework, a roadmap, and a daily companion. It guides you through four powerful phases—Connect, Heal, Build, and Thrive—so that every choice, every breath, and every ritual draws you closer to living in alignment with your soul's deepest calling.

Phase One: Connect—Awakening to Your Divine Source

At the heart of every human being lies a spark of divinity—a limitless source of love, wisdom, and guidance. Yet, in the busyness of life, this sacred presence can feel distant and seemingly unreachable. Connect is about reclaiming that closeness. It is a conscious act of opening yourself to the truth you have always known: you are whole and you are loved.

Connection is not a fleeting moment of prayer or a quiet pause in the day. It's a relationship, a steady, ongoing dialogue with your higher self, your intuition, and the universal energy that flows through all things. When you cultivate this connection, you begin to notice the subtle signals that your body, mind, and spirit have been sending all along. Your heart softens, your mind clears, and inspiration finds you with greater ease.

Practices to cultivate connection:

1. **Daily meditation:** Begin with five minutes. Sit quietly, breathe deeply, and visualize your heart opening like a flower, receiving love, guidance, and peace.
2. **Reflective journaling:** Ask yourself, "What do I need today? What brings me joy?" This simple act strengthens self-awareness and deepens spiritual connection.
3. **Nature immersion:** Step outside. Listen to the wind, feel the grass beneath your feet, watch the sunlight dance through the trees. Let the world remind you of your place in the infinite. Dance with your ancestors.
4. **Gratitude practice:** Every day, acknowledge three things you are grateful for. Gratitude aligns you with abundance and invites joy into your life.

When you prioritize connection, healing begins effortlessly. Your energy becomes magnetic. Your choices are clearer. Your life starts to feel aligned, purposeful, and expansive.

Phase Two: Heal—Releasing the Past, Restoring Your Mind

Once connection is established, the next step is Heal. Healing is not about fixing something broken; it's about lighting up the shadows in your mind, your heart, and your emotions. It's the act of acknowledging your pain, releasing limiting beliefs, and nurturing self-compassion.

Healing is not a one-time event. The mind is a storyteller, often replaying old wounds or imagining future anxieties. Without conscious healing, these patterns can shape how we show up in relationships, work, and life itself.

Tools for healing:

1. **Mindfulness and awareness:** Observe your thoughts without judgment. Notice patterns that no longer serve you, and redirect your focus to what nourishes your soul.
2. **Emotional release techniques:** Journaling, breathwork, and somatic exercises enable stored emotions to move. Cry, laugh, shake—whatever your body needs to release is sacred.
3. **Self-compassion practices:** Speak to yourself as you would a dear friend. Replace criticism with encouragement. Recognize that your worth is inherent, not earned.
4. **Therapeutic support:** Healing is not meant to be solitary. Seek coaches, therapists, or guides to navigate trauma or challenging patterns.

Through healing, you create space—space for clarity, empowerment, and peace. Your past no longer dictates your future; your present choices do.

Phase Three: Build—Strengthening Body, Mind, and Energy

With connection and healing being nurtured, it's time to Build. This phase is about honoring your body, strengthening your mind, and cultivating sustainable energy. Your body is a sacred vessel, your mind a powerful tool, and your energy a currency that must be managed wisely.

Nourishing the body:

1. **Nutrition for vitality:** Whole, nutrient-rich foods provide energy and clarity. Mindful eating deepens your connection with your body.
2. **Movement as medicine:** Exercise is celebration, not punishment. Gentle yoga, walks, or strength training energize and cultivate presence.

3. **Rest and recovery:** Sleep is a cornerstone. Respect your body's need for pause and rejuvenation.
4. **Rituals of care:** Morning stretches, evening baths, lighting candles with intention. Try small acts that tell your nervous system that you are worthy of care and you are safe.

Mental and energetic practices are equally important in this phase. Learn to set boundaries, prioritize your energy, and align your actions with your purpose. When mind, body, and energy are strengthened, thriving becomes inevitable.

Phase Four: Thrive—Living a Purpose-Driven Life

The final phase, Thrive, is the culmination of connection, healing, and building. Thriving is not a checklist; it's a state of being. It's living aligned with your passions, expressing your authentic self, nurturing deep relationships, managing resources wisely, and contributing meaningfully to the world.

Thriving in daily life:

1. **Purposeful living:** Align your actions with what lights you up; passion, talent, and soul calling.
2. **Relationship mastery:** Surround yourself with those who elevate and inspire you. Practice empathy, communication, and boundaries.
3. **Financial empowerment:** Manage resources intentionally. Release scarcity thinking. Invite abundance.
4. **Contribution and legacy:** Your impact amplifies your fulfillment. Whether through service, mentorship, or creativity, your contributions honor your life.

Thriving is not about perfection. It is about showing up fully, cocreating your life with intention, and stepping into the flow of abundance, clarity, and joy.

Integrating the Seven Areas of Wellbeing

The CHBT Method is holistic. It touches seven interconnected areas of wellbeing: spiritual, emotional, mental, nutritional, physical, social, and financial. Nurturing one amplifies the others. When alignment is achieved across these areas, your life radiates harmony, purpose and peace.

Your Invitation to Transformation

This method is not a quick fix; it is a journey. It invites you to slow down, reflect, and practice daily rituals that bring your life into alignment. Those who commit to it notice the following results:

- Greater clarity and insight
- Emotional resilience
- Energy and vitality
- Deep, fulfilling relationships
- Alignment with divine guidance

Wellbeing is not a destination, it's a state of being and a return to yourself.

The invitation is simple: Commit to yourself. Show up for your mind, body, spirit, and purpose. Begin small. Stay consistent. Allow these rituals to ripple into every corner of your life.

This is your opportunity to live aligned, intentional, and liberated. Your journey begins with one conscious breath, one intentional choice and one sacred ritual at a time.

The Black Butterfly

Tohamina / Freepik

Source: https://share.google/kgkC1Clq0A4H1jWzJ.

The black butterfly is a symbol of transformation in its most profound and sacred form. While butterflies have long represented rebirth and renewal, the black butterfly carries a deeper message: one of mystery, power and the beauty that can emerge from our shadow. It invites us to honor not only the light we embody but also the darkness we move through on our journey toward wholeness.

In many cultures, the black butterfly appears during moments of transition—when the soul is shedding what no longer serves and preparing to step into a higher state of being. It reminds us that healing and transformation are not always soft or effortless; they often unfold in the quiet, hidden spaces where we must trust without seeing. Like the cocoon, those moments of stillness, uncertainty and surrender are where our most powerful metamorphoses occur.

Black, as a color, carries both elegance and depth. It absorbs light rather than reflecting it, symbolizing introspection, grounding, and the ability to hold all experiences (joy and pain, clarity and confusion) without judgment. The black butterfly, therefore, becomes an emblem of sustainable transformation: the kind that doesn't rush or seek perfection, but rather evolves with grace, patience, and self-awareness.

A month after my mother transitioned, I experienced this symbolism in the most profound way. I was speaking with friends in my backyard, still deep in grief, when a black butterfly appeared. She fluttered around me, then gently landed on my shoulder. She returned three times, each time resting on me with a stillness that felt like a kiss; a whisper from beyond that said, "I'm here. I've only changed form." In that moment, I knew it was her. The black butterfly had become her messenger, a sacred bridge between worlds, reminding me that love never dies; it only transforms.

For me, the black butterfly became a living symbol of hope, presence, and the infinite continuity of life. It taught me that even in the darkest moments, there is beauty waiting to be recognized. Its wings, soft yet strong, mirror the resilience that lives within us—the quiet power to rise again, renewed and radiant, after the storms of life have passed.

For this reason, the black butterfly serves as a perfect guide for your journey with this book. As you begin each chapter, may this butterfly remind you that true wellbeing is not about perfection or constant light, but about harmony: the sustainable luxury of living in alignment with learning from the shadows as you embody your highest and most sacred self. This book is your cocoon.

1 Spiritual Wellbeing

Tohamina / Freepik

Healing Your Relationship with God Is Healing Your Relationship with Yourself

Spiritual freedom begins when you give yourself permission to let go of who the world told you to be and return to who your soul already knows you are.

In this chapter, I use the words *God*, *Spirit*, and the *Divine* interchangeably, as they all point to the same universal source of love, wisdom, and healing.

When I look back on the moments in my life when I've felt the most peace, alignment, and love, it's always been during times I was deeply connected to Spirit.

I'll be honest, though; this wasn't always the case. There were times I questioned everything about that connection. Was it real? Was I talking to something outside myself or just hoping the universe would validate me? Through my spiritual practice, I've learned something profound: healing my relationship with Spirit is really about healing my relationship with myself.

I'm not talking about God limited to religious rules or texts. I'm talking about what I grew to understand as the Holy Spirit, which I now call Spirit, the Divine presence that whispers through the trees, moves with the wind, and flows through my veins. It's that undeniable sense of connection to something greater, something that nurtures me beyond words. When I nurture that connection, everything in life feels blessed.

My Story: Rediscovering Divine Connection

Let me take you back to a time when I was struggling. I was doing all the "right" things: eating well, practicing yoga, meditating, and reciting affirmations daily . . . but something felt off. Deep down, I wasn't fully aligned in all areas of my life.

Then one day, during meditation, it hit me. I'd been so focused on external wellbeing that I neglected the most important part: my spirit. I forgot to nurture my relationship with God—not in a religious sense, but in a deeply personal way. True healing begins from within, and it starts with that divine connection. I was spending most of my time doing instead of being. Practicing but not listening.

So, I sat in stillness and prayed for divine guidance. I didn't ask for anything. I simply surrendered, released control, and knew I didn't have all the answers. At that moment, something shifted. It was like a door opening inside myself, one that had been closed for so long. On the other side was peace; not loud or overwhelming, but a quiet knowing that I was exactly where I needed to be and that it was time to fully surrender to divine guidance in every area of my life.

That's the thing about spiritual wellbeing: when you truly connect, you realize you are worthy—worthy of love, healing, and everything you've been searching for. You stop seeking external validation because you understand the only validation that matters comes from within. It's already there, waiting for you to recognize it. Your soul knows exactly what you need.

> *"Your healing begins the moment you remember you were never broken—only disconnected from the wholeness that has always lived within you."*

The Benefits of Nurturing Your Relationship with Spirit

Research shows spirituality profoundly influences mental and emotional wellbeing. In a large meta-analysis, Yaden and colleagues (2022) found that spirituality is consistently associated with greater life satisfaction and overall wellbeing.

Those who engage regularly in spiritual practices experience less depression and anxiety. According to the Pew Research Center (2017), about 80% of Americans believe in God or a higher power and credit these beliefs for their peace and fulfillment.

Spiritual rituals lead to the following results:

- **Increased resilience:** Spirit nurtures hope and purpose during crisis.
- **Enhanced emotional regulation:** Connection to the Divine helps manage emotions and stress.
- **Greater sense of community:** Spirituality builds supportive networks.

This journey requires vulnerability and letting go of old beliefs that no longer serve you. But when you commit to nurturing your relationship with Spirit, you'll see yourself differently (as perfect, whole, and complete), even mistakes and misalignments become divine teachers.

For many, connecting with God or Spirit can feel overwhelming. Maybe you've been told there's only one "right" way or you've been hurt by past religious experiences. Here's what I want you to know: There is no one right way. Your connection with God, Spirit, or the Divine is as unique as you are and doesn't have to look like anyone else's.

For me, connection comes through pranayama, prayer, water, meditation, and nature. The stillness of early morning, the sunrise lighting the world—these remind me of God's love. No matter how dark life gets, the sun shines again. During many "dark nights of the soul," observing nature grounds me. In those moments, I feel connected, aligned, and at peace.

> *"There comes a point in life where you realize if you don't start loving your way through, you're not gonna make it through, and the first person you have to start loving most is you."*

Your connection might look different: the rhythm of your breath, a favorite song, quiet moments before sleep, your children's laughter, the sun on your skin, or your heartbeat. However you connect, trust that it's enough. Trust that *you* are enough.

This isn't about perfection; it's about alignment, nurturing the most important relationship you'll ever have: with your soul, with Spirit . . . with God. When you do, everything else begins to fall into place.

Healing Through Connection

Healing isn't about fixing what's broken. It's about remembering who you truly are: whole, healed, and deeply loved.

When you heal your relationship with God, you heal your relationship with yourself. You realize you are not separate from the Divine; you are part of it. This realization unlocks peace, joy, and profound healing.

Daily Ritual: Nurturing Your Connection with Spirit

Divine Connection Meditation

1. **Find your space:** Choose a quiet, comfortable place to sit or lie down without distractions.
2. **Set an intention:** Close your eyes and set an intention, such as "I open my heart to divine guidance."

3. **Breathe deeply:** Inhale through your nose, exhale through your mouth. Feel your body relax with each breath.
4. **Visualize your connection:** Imagine a warm light surrounding you, the love and presence of Spirit. Feel it embrace you with peace and warmth.
5. **Listen and surrender:** Sit in silence, observing thoughts without judgment. If your mind wanders, gently return focus to the breath.
6. **Affirm your worth:** Silently or aloud, say the following:
   - "I am worthy of love."
   - "I am connected to Spirit."
   - "I am whole and complete."
7. **Close the meditation:** Slowly bring awareness back—wiggle your fingers and toes and open your eyes when you're ready.
8. **Reflect:** Notice how you feel and consider journaling any insights.

"Every ritual is a doorway—a way back to your breath, your body, your soul, and the infinite love that holds it all."

Practice this meditation daily to deepen your connection and invite healing.

Seven Spiritual Wellbeing Rituals

Here are simple, accessible rituals grounded in ancient wisdom and modern science. Whether you have 5 minutes or 50, a quiet space or a chaotic household, these practices invite love, alignment, and healing into your daily life.

Intentional Affirmations Ritual

There is a lot of talk about the power of affirmations. But, what are they? And do they actually work or are they just feel-good words we repeat to ourselves in the mirror? I am here to demystify affirmations and invite you to amplify them because they are more than just words: they are a profound tool to rewire your mind, reshape your reality, and realign your energy with your deepest desires.

Affirmations are declarations of your inner truth. When spoken with intention, they are a bridge between your current reality and the life you are consciously choosing to create. Think of them not as empty statements, but as seeds planted in the fertile soil of your subconscious mind. Over time, these seeds grow into the beliefs, habits, and experiences that reflect your highest self.

I have seen the transformative power of affirmations firsthand, not just in my life but in the lives of thousands of clients I have guided through spiritual and personal growth practices. I have witnessed individuals who once doubted themselves, who felt stuck in cycles of negativity or self-sabotage, gradually shift their mindset, attract abundance, and step confidently into their purpose, all through the simple, yet powerful practice of speaking intentional affirmations.

So how do affirmations really work? At the core, affirmations work because our thoughts and words are vibrational. Every word we speak carries energy, and when aligned with intention, this energy communicates directly with our subconscious mind. The subconscious does not differentiate between reality and imagination; it accepts repeated statements as truth. This is why a consistent, intentional affirmation practice has the power to shift beliefs, reprogram mental patterns, and, ultimately, change your life.

But here's the key: Affirmations are most effective when they are intentional, personalized, and emotionally charged. Generic affirmations like "I am happy" or "I am successful" can have some effect, but when you craft affirmations that resonate deeply with your own soul and reflect your inner desires, they become transformative. The goal is not just to say words, but to speak from a place of inner knowing and intention.

Let me walk you through my signature process for creating personalized affirmations. The first step is self-reflection. Take a moment to ask yourself, "What do I need to hear from myself? What limiting beliefs do I carry that no longer serve me? What qualities, experiences or energies am I ready to invite into my life?" Your answers to these questions will guide the creation of affirmations that truly speak to your soul.

Once you identify your core needs, frame them in the present tense, as if they are already true. The subconscious responds best to statements that are definitive and grounded in the now. For example, rather than saying, "I will be confident someday," you might affirm, "I am confident and courageous in every area of my life." The difference may seem subtle, but it's profound. Present-tense affirmations bypass doubt and resistance and enable your mind to align with the energy of the reality you are creating.

Next, add emotional intensity. The power of an affirmation is amplified when you feel it in your body as you speak it. Notice how your energy shifts when you declare something that resonates with your heart. This emotional connection bridges the gap between words and manifestation. Pair your affirmations with deep, mindful breathing or gentle movement to embody the energy fully.

Here are seven examples of affirmations that I often recommend:

- **"I am worthy of love and success."** This affirmation counters feelings of unworthiness. It reminds you that you deserve to achieve your goals, experience joy, and receive love, from both others and yourself. Over time, repeating this affirmation can help dissolve self-doubt and cultivate self-compassion.
- **"I embrace change and trust the process."** Life is full of uncertainty and change can often feel uncomfortable. By affirming your trust in the process, you cultivate resilience and openness. This affirmation helps you navigate transitions with grace, inviting new opportunities while releasing fear and resistance.
- **"I trust my body's sacred wisdom."** Our bodies are sacred vessels, deeply connected to Spirit. This affirmation invites you to listen to your body as a guide, honoring its messages about rest, nourishment, and healing. By affirming your trust, you strengthen the bond between body and soul, and create space for greater alignment and vitality.
- **"I attract positivity and abundance into my life."** Affirmations of abundance align your energy with prosperity. They shift your focus from scarcity to gratitude, enabling you to notice and invite opportunities for growth, connection, and fulfillment.
- **"I deserve the best life has to offer."** This affirmation is a powerful reminder of your inherent worthiness. Too often, people unconsciously settle for less—in relationships, careers, or self-care—because of limiting beliefs about what they "deserve." Declaring that you are worthy of life's fullness and joy affirms that you are open to receiving blessings, opportunities, and love in their highest form. It shifts your energy from merely surviving to fully thriving.
- **"I am capable of achieving my dreams and living my purpose."** This affirmation strengthens self-belief and motivation. It reminds

you of your innate potential and empowers you to take aligned action toward your aspirations, reinforcing the truth that you are capable of extraordinary things.

- **"I am divinely guided and supported in all that I do."** This affirmation anchors your practice in Spirit. It reminds you that you are never walking alone, that divine wisdom is always available, and that even in times of uncertainty, you are held, guided, and supported by a higher power.

The beauty of affirmations is that they are versatile. They can be spoken aloud in front of a mirror, written in a journal, whispered during meditation, or even recorded and played back as a daily reminder. I often encourage clients to create a dedicated ritual space for their affirmations, a quiet and sacred corner where they can focus without distractions. Pairing your affirmations with intentional lighting, calming scents, or soft music can deepen their impact and make the practice feel like a true spiritual ritual.

One of my favorite stories involves a client who had struggled with self-esteem and chronic self-doubt for years. We crafted affirmations specifically for her insecurities and she practiced them daily, in the morning and evening. Over a few months, she noticed subtle but profound changes: She began speaking more confidently at work, pursuing opportunities she had previously avoided, and forming healthier relationships. Her life shifted not because of luck, but because her energy and mindset aligned with her affirmations. This is the power of intentional words—they shape not only your thoughts but your experiences and interactions with the world.

It's normal if your affirmations feel untrue at first. Think of them as seeds planted in the fertile soil of your mind. You're not forcing belief instantly; you're gradually retraining your brain and shifting your energy. Repetition, emotion, and reflection are the nutrients that help these seeds grow.

Remember, affirmations are not magic in isolation. They are a powerful tool when paired with aligned action reflection and inner work. They serve as a compass, guiding you toward your highest self, but you still have to take inspired steps to manifest your vision. Think of affirmations as both a declaration and an invitation: You declare the truth of your desires and you invite the universe to support you in bringing them into reality.

I encourage you to experiment with your affirmations, observe how they make you feel, and refine them as your journey unfolds. Your needs, goals, and desires will evolve and your affirmations should evolve with them. What matters most is consistency, intention, and the emotional resonance behind each statement.

By integrating an intentional affirmations ritual into your daily life, you are not only nurturing your spiritual wellbeing but you are also consciously shaping the life you want to live. Every word you speak with purpose carries energy, every repetition strengthens your belief, and every alignment brings you closer to your deepest truth.

Affirmations are not just self-help tools; they are sacred practices that honor your inner wisdom, your desires, and your divine potential. When embraced fully, they have the power to transform your mindset, elevate your energy, and ultimately create a life that reflects the highest version of yourself.

From a scientific perspective, affirmations work through neuroplasticity: the brain's ability to rewire itself based on repeated thought patterns. Each time you speak an empowering statement, you're strengthening new neural pathways while dissolving old loops of fear, doubt, and unworthiness. Spiritually, you are attuning your energy field to the frequency of your desired reality, embodying the vibration of what you wish to attract before it manifests.

This ritual bridges science and soul, grounding the mystical power of intention in proven psychology and energetic alignment.

Now that you understand how affirmations rewire the mind and attune your energy, let's bring this into practice with a simple, three-step ritual designed to make your words come alive.

Step 1: Self-Reflection Take a few quiet breaths. Place your hand over your heart and ask, "What do I need to hear from myself right now?" Identify the beliefs that limit your light and gently release them. This is the clearing—the fertile ground for new truth to take root.

Step 2: Present-Tense Power Affirmations work best when spoken as if they are already true. Speak in the now; your subconscious doesn't know the difference between imagination and reality. When you affirm, "I am," you are commanding your energy into form.

> *"The most sacred journey you will ever take is from fear to faith, from self-doubt to self-love, and from searching outside yourself to finding love within."*

Step 3: Feel It Fully Emotion is the activator. Feel your affirmation in your body. Breathe it into your cells. Let your tone rise with conviction and your energy expand as if the words are wrapping around you like light.

Speak them out loud, whisper them in meditation, or write them in your journal. Pair your practice with candlelight, soft music, or the scent of essential oils.

This is not just repetition; it's recalibration.

Every word becomes a step toward your evolution.

Nature Prayer Walk Ritual

There is something profoundly healing about stepping outside, leaving behind the noise of the world, and immersing yourself in the living, breathing sanctuary of nature. When you walk with Spirit in nature, you are reminded of what has always been true: you are part of creation, not separate from it. The trees breathe with you. The wind carries messages if you listen. The ground beneath your feet holds you steady, as it has held humanity for generations. However, you don't need to travel far (or even stand) to experience this ritual. Whether walking, seated, or imagining a natural space, you can cultivate presence, prayer, and connection to Spirit. To that end, I have included accessibility and mobility options in this section.

A Nature Prayer Walk is more than just exercise or fresh air. It is a spiritual practice, a walking meditation, a prayer in motion, an opportunity to tune your heart to the rhythm of the Divine. By walking slowly, intentionally, and prayerfully, you enable yourself to hear Spirit not in words but in sensations, whispers, and symbols from the natural world.

I can't count the number of times I've gone on a prayer walk carrying heaviness, confusion, or unanswered questions and returned with clarity, peace, and sometimes a message so direct I could only call it a Divine download. Spirit speaks through creation if we are willing to listen.

From a scientific perspective, walking in nature activates the parasympathetic nervous system, lowering cortisol and easing anxiety. Studies from

Stanford University (Bratman et al., 2015) show that spending time in green spaces decreases rumination (the repetitive thought loops linked to stress and depression) while increasing creative flow and emotional regulation. Spiritually, nature is a mirror of divine intelligence. When we walk prayerfully, we don't just observe creation; we merge with it.

Why Nature Prayer Walks Work Modern science supports what mystics and sages have known for centuries: time in nature is medicine. Research published in the *Proceedings of the National Academy of Sciences* (Bratman et al., 2015) found that people who spent even short periods of time walking in nature had reduced rumination—the kind of repetitive, negative thought cycles that often lead to anxiety and depression. Brain scans revealed decreased activity in the subgenual prefrontal cortex, the region linked to mental distress.

In other words, when you walk in nature, your brain literally shifts into a calmer, more restorative state.

Research consistently shows that time spent in nature lowers stress hormones, reduces blood pressure, improves mood and cognitive functioning, and fosters feelings of connectedness and meaning (Bratman et al., 2019).

When you combine the grounding power of nature with prayer and presence, you create a sacred container for transformation.

How to Practice a Nature Prayer Walk

1. **Choose your space:** You don't need a forest or mountain trail for this ritual to work. A local park, a quiet neighborhood street lined with trees, or even your backyard can become holy ground. The key is to choose a place where you feel safe, comfortable, and able to walk without constant interruption.
2. **Set an intention or prayer:** Begin your walk by pausing in stillness. Place your hands over your heart, take a few deep breaths, and offer a simple prayer. You might ask:
   - "Spirit, what do I need to understand today?"
   - "God, how can I see Your presence more clearly in my life?"
   - "Divine, show me what I need to release and what I need to embrace."

   This sets the tone, turning an ordinary walk into a sacred dialogue.

3. **Walk in silence:** Resist the urge to bring headphones, podcasts, or phone calls into this space. The goal is not distraction, but presence. Silence opens the channel to Spirit. As you walk, slow your pace enough to notice the details around you, the way the light filters through leaves, the rhythm of your footsteps, the sound of birds calling to one another.
4. **Observe with sacred attention:** Every element of nature can be a teacher. The resilience of a tree may remind you of your own strength. The way a stream flows effortlessly around rocks may speak to your need for surrender. The warmth of the sun might feel like God's love resting on your skin. Open your senses fully: Touch the bark; smell the air; notice textures, colors, and patterns.
5. **Listen and receive:** After some time observing, bring your awareness inward. What thoughts are surfacing? What emotions are present? Do any symbols or images stand out to you? Sometimes Spirit's messages arrive as an inner knowing, other times through synchronicities like a butterfly crossing your path at the exact moment you asked for reassurance. Trust what comes.
6. **Close with gratitude:** Before ending your walk, pause again in stillness. Offer thanks for whatever insights or feelings arose, even if they are subtle. Gratitude seals the ritual and honors the partnership with you, Spirit, and creation.
7. **Reflect:** After your walk, consider journaling. Write down what you noticed, what you felt, and any answers or impressions you received. Over time, you may notice patterns or recurring messages, Spirit's way of guiding you with consistency.

Accessibility/Limited Mobility Options For readers who cannot walk long distances or at all, try these stationary or seated alternatives:

- **Seated nature prayer:** Sit on a porch, balcony, or near a window with a view of trees, sky, or garden. Follow the same intention setting, observation, listening, and gratitude steps while seated.
- **Indoor nature prayer:** Use plants, flowers, or natural objects indoors. Move your hands gently over leaves, feel textures, or gaze mindfully at natural light.

- **Guided visualization:** Imagine a walk through a natural space. Engage all senses—hear the birds, feel the wind, smell the flowers. Pair with affirmations and deep breathing.

My Story of Healing Through Nature Prayer Walks There was a time in my life when I felt overwhelmed by decisions, torn between staying on a safe path and leaping into my deeper purpose. I prayed, journaled, and meditated, but clarity eluded me. One morning, I felt nudged to go for a walk in a nearby park. I left my phone behind and simply put out an invitation to God for Spirit to lead me. It's become my favorite invitation since I heard the song "Oceans (Where Feet May Fail)" by Hillsong United.

As I walked, I noticed a river flowing beside me. At one point, the water split into two streams: one shallow and rocky, the other wide and smooth. For some reason, I stopped there. It was as if Spirit whispered, "Which flow do you want to follow: the path of struggle or the path of surrender?" I knew in that moment what choice I needed to make.

That day changed me. The decision became easy because I realized I wasn't choosing alone. Spirit was guiding me, not with words, but through nature's wisdom. Since then, prayer walks and time in nature have become a non-negotiable part of my spiritual wellbeing practice.

Why This Ritual Is Transformative

- **Grounds you in the present:** Walking without distraction anchors you in the here and now, dissolving stress and overthinking.
- **Strengthens your intuition:** Nature quiets the noise of the world so you can hear the whispers of your soul more clearly.
- **Deepens your connection to spirit:** Creation becomes a living scripture, revealing God's presence in every detail.
- **Restores balance:** By aligning your body, mind, and spirit through movement and prayer, you return to a natural rhythm of peace.

Affirmations for Your Nature Walk To enhance your ritual, you may repeat affirmations silently as you walk. Some examples:

- "I walk in harmony with Spirit."
- "Every step connects me to Divine wisdom."

- "The Earth supports me, Spirit guides me, and I am never alone."
- "With each breath, I release fear and receive peace."

The next time you feel restless, heavy, or disconnected, step outside. Take a few mindful breaths. Begin walking with prayer in your heart. Let the wind, the trees, the sunlight, and the earth remind you that Spirit is always speaking. When you walk with sacred attention, even the simplest path becomes holy ground.

> *"Peace is not found in the absence of challenges but in the presence of trust. Trust in God, trust in the process, trust in your ability to surrender to your greatest and highest good."*

Your Nature Prayer Walk is not about reaching a destination. It's about realizing you were never separate from the Divine in the first place. Every step is communion, every breath is prayer, and every moment in creation is an invitation to remember who you truly are.

Manifestation Meditation Ritual

Manifestation is not about chasing what's missing; it's about aligning with what's already meant for you. The Manifestation Meditation Ritual bridges the gap between imagination and reality, helping you embody your highest self and magnetize the life you desire through conscious visualization, emotion, and energetic alignment.

From a scientific perspective, visualization has been shown to activate the same neural pathways as physical action. In a landmark study (Driskell et al., 1994), researchers found that mental imagery enhances performance by strengthening the brain's belief in what is possible, essentially training your mind to expect success. Spiritually, this practice is the art of becoming vibrationally compatible with your vision. When your inner frequency matches your desire, manifestation moves from potential to presence.

This ritual merges the science of neuroplasticity with the soul of divine creation, inviting you to remember that your imagination is one of your most sacred tools.

Step 1: Set the Scene Find a peaceful space where you can sit comfortably. Light a candle, burn sage or incense, or simply close your eyes and breathe. Create an environment that feels like an energetic sanctuary—one that mirrors the peace of your future self.

Step 2: Ground and Center Place your hand over your heart and take slow, intentional breaths. With each inhale, draw in calm. With each exhale, release resistance. Feel your body soften as you prepare to meet your higher self.

Step 3: Visualize Your Highest Self See yourself living the life you desire: radiant, grounded, and aligned. Imagine every detail: how you move, how you feel, the people around you, the environment you've created. Let the vision become vivid in color, sound, and emotion.

Step 4: Call In Your Desires Silently affirm: "I am open to receiving what is meant for me." Picture your desires as light surrounding you—already yours, already unfolding. Feel the gratitude and joy as if it has already happened.

Step 5: Seal It with Surrender Release attachment to the outcome. Whisper a prayer of trust: "May this or something even greater manifest for my highest good."

This ritual trains the mind to believe, the heart to receive, and the soul to align.

When thought, feeling, and faith merge, manifestation becomes meditation in motion.

My Story of Manifestation in Motion I remember reading Yvonne Orji's book *Bamboozled by Jesus* and being inspired by how she visualized every detail of the home she wanted. That concept stayed with me. At the time, I was living in a beautiful ocean-view apartment in Marina del Rey, California (a manifestation I shared about in my first book, *Let Your Fears Make You Fierce*), but I realized that instead of wasting money on rent, I could consciously level up.

I allowed myself to imagine a house that felt perfectly aligned with my highest self: a spacious home with a saltwater pool, a cozy fireplace, an island kitchen, and light-filled rooms that welcomed love, peace, and creativity.

I visualized every detail; the way sunlight would hit the living room in the morning, the sound of water flowing in the pool, the feeling of cooking meals in my dream kitchen.

At the time, I thought the only thing holding me back was being married. Instead of letting that stop me, I leaned fully into visualization. I imagined living in that home, walking through it, feeling the joy of each space, and trusting that the universe would bring me into alignment with it.

Fast forward: that exact home—the one I saw in my mind so clearly—became my reality in Atlanta, Georgia. I realized then that the power of manifestation isn't about wishful thinking; it's about aligning your energy with the reality you are ready to receive.

Life Visioning, a practice I learned from Reverend Micheal Bernard Beckwith at Agape, taught me to recognize opportunities, make aligned decisions, and embody the life I desire. The meditation didn't just create the home; it shifted my frequency so that the home could find me.

Gratitude Prayer Ritual

Gratitude is one of the most potent medicines for the mind and soul. The Gratitude Prayer Ritual transforms simple appreciation into a sacred daily practice—an evening reflection that reconnects you to the abundance already flowing through your life.

Research by psychologists Emmons and McCullough (2003) reveals that individuals who kept gratitude journals reported higher levels of optimism, better sleep, fewer physical complaints, and a deeper sense of connection to life. Gratitude literally reshapes the brain, activating the prefrontal cortex (associated with positive emotion and decision-making) and quieting the amygdala, the center of fear and stress.

Spiritually, gratitude is a prayer of remembrance. It whispers, "I have enough, I am enough, and all is well." When we end the day in thankfulness, we calibrate our energy to receive even more blessings.

Step 1: Create Sacred Space As the sun sets, light a candle or sit by a window where you can see the fading light. Take a few slow breaths and let the day soften around you. Feel the shift from doing to being, from striving to surrendering.

Step 2: Reflect on Three to Five Blessings Close your eyes and recall three to five things you're grateful for from the day. They don't have to be grand: a smile from a stranger, a nourishing meal, a moment of peace. What matters is presence. Gratitude amplifies when it's specific and felt deeply.

Step 3: Speak a Prayer of Thanks With hands over your heart, whisper a simple prayer: "Thank you for the love that guided me today. Thank you for the lessons that shaped me. Thank you for the breath that sustains me."

Let each word carry warmth and sincerity; this is how gratitude moves from the mind to the soul.

Step 4: Feel and Release Pause and allow the feeling of gratitude to expand in your body. Imagine golden light radiating from your heart, wrapping you in peace. Exhale any lingering worry or tension; you are safe, supported, and loved.

Step 5: Rest in Grace End your practice by journaling your blessings or simply saying, "Thank you for this day." Let gratitude be your lullaby.

This ritual unites the science of happiness with the soul of prayer.

When you close each day in gratitude, you don't just count blessings, you become one.

My Story of Gratitude in Action I remember a night when I was feeling restless and overwhelmed, unsure if my efforts were making a difference because of back-to-back losses in my personal and professional life. I started to spiral and think of all the things I could've done better until I realized I was beating myself up pretty bad.

I paused and allowed myself to reflect on the day. I started small: a client's breakthrough session, a nourishing meal I had prepared for my husband, the sound of rain nourishing the land. As I named each blessing, I felt my heart soften and the tension in my shoulders melting away. By the time I finished my prayer of thanks, I noticed a profound shift—my worries seemed lighter, my perspective clearer, and my heart warmer. That evening reminded me that gratitude isn't just a ritual; it's a bridge back to presence and alignment. Even in moments of doubt, it reconnects you to the abundance that surrounds you.

Pranayama Ritual

The breath is Spirit in motion. It is the first gift we receive when we arrive on this Earth and the final offering we release when we leave. Between those two sacred moments, breath becomes the invisible thread that connects body to soul, science to divinity, and consciousness to creation.

The Pranayama Ritual honors this truth. Pranayama, from the Sanskrit *prana* (life force) and *ayama* (extension or regulation), is the ancient art of consciously directing life energy through breath. To breathe with awareness is to dance with Spirit, to remember that you are both physical and divine, grounded and infinite.

Science confirms what the sages always knew. Research by Brown and Gerbarg (2005) demonstrates that rhythmic breathing can regulate the autonomic nervous system, lower stress hormones, and increase heart rate variability, a key marker of resilience and emotional balance. Slow, intentional breath patterns also activate the parasympathetic response, calming the body while enhancing clarity and focus.

Spiritually, every inhale is a moment of receiving—an act of trust that the universe will provide what you need. Every exhale is a surrender, a release of control, tension, and fear. Through this rhythm, breath becomes prayer.

Step 1: Create Stillness Find a quiet space where your body can relax and your awareness can expand. Sit comfortably with your spine tall. Close your eyes. Let your breath flow naturally for a few moments, simply noticing its rhythm.

Step 2: Set Your Intention Whisper silently, "With each breath, I connect more deeply to Spirit." Let this intention guide your practice, transforming every inhale and exhale into a conscious act of remembrance.

Step 3: Practice Conscious Breathing Inhale slowly through the nose for a count of four, allowing your belly to expand. Hold for a count of two. Exhale through the mouth or nose for a count of six, feeling the release. Repeat this cycle for 5 to 10 rounds.

You may choose to explore alternate nostril breathing (*Nadi Shodhana*) to balance energy or box breathing (4-4-4-4) to calm the mind.

Step 4: Feel Spirit Move Through You Notice the subtle change: your heart steadying, your thoughts slowing, your energy grounding. Feel the sacred exchange of life force flowing through every cell.

Step 5: Close with Gratitude Rest your hands over your heart and say quietly, "Thank you, Breath, for being my constant companion, my first teacher, my final peace, and my living prayer."

When you breathe with intention, you remember who you are: *a vessel of Spirit, sustained by the rhythm of life itself.*

My Story of Breath and Stress A few years ago, I started tracking my stress levels with my Oura Ring. I was shocked to see that I was spending seven to eight hours a day in high-stress states. My body constantly signaled tension, even when I thought I was managing. I realized I had normalized stress and had no idea the toll it was taking on my body.

I decided to intentionally integrate seven sacred breaths anytime my ring indicated I was stressed. Within weeks, the shift was undeniable: My daily stress dropped from seven to eight hours to less than three hours a day. It wasn't just numbers on a screen; I could feel the difference in my body, my clarity, and my emotional resilience. Breath became my anchor, my instant reset, and my tangible proof that conscious inhalation and exhalation can transform the way we navigate life.

Frequency Activation Ritual

Sound is creation. Every vibration carries information, and every frequency holds power. Long before words were spoken, the universe sang itself into being; galaxies unfolding through resonance, energy, and rhythm. The Frequency Activation Ritual is a remembrance of that truth: that we, too, are made of vibration, and we can tune ourselves to higher frequencies of harmony, clarity, and love.

From a scientific lens, sound healing aligns with the principles of entrainment: the process by which rhythmic vibrations synchronize biological rhythms such as heart rate, breath, and brainwave activity. Research by Lehrer and Gevirtz (2014) on resonance frequency breathing and biofeedback shows that rhythmic sound and controlled breathing can regulate the autonomic nervous system, increasing heart rate variability and reducing anxiety.

Spiritually, sound is medicine. Whether through mantra, music, or the deep hum of a Tibetan bowl, frequency bypasses the mind and speaks directly to the soul. When you intentionally activate sound, you become a tuning fork for peace, realigning your inner world with the universal rhythm of the earth.

Step 1: Prepare Your Sacred Sanctuary Choose a peaceful space where sound can flow freely. You may want to play binaural beats to balance brain hemispheres, or Solfeggio frequencies, ancient tonal patterns believed to restore energetic harmony (396 Hz for liberation, 528 Hz for transformation, 639 Hz for connection, 852 Hz for awakening). Light a candle, sit comfortably, and invite stillness.

Step 2: Set an Intention for Resonance Whisper your desire into the space. It could be peace, clarity, healing, or expansion. Let your intention become the note you wish to carry.

Step 3: Activate the Frequency Begin your sound ritual:

- Play music tuned to 432 Hz, the "heartbeat of the Earth."
- Activate a crystal sound bowl and let the vibration ripple through you.
- Chant a mantra such as "om," "so hum," or "I am light" to align your inner voice with cosmic rhythm.

Breathe deeply in time with the sound. Feel how the vibration shifts the energy in your body, loosening tension, clearing stagnation, and awakening flow.

Step 4: Feel the Harmony Notice how your body becomes an instrument—each cell pulsing, each inhale harmonizing. The sound doesn't come to you; it moves through you. You are the frequency.

Step 5: Seal with Silence and Gratitude When the sound fades, rest in the silence that follows. This is integration, where the vibration settles and transformation begins. Whisper a prayer of thanks for the energy awakened within you.

This ritual unites the science of resonance with the soul of remembrance.

When you align with divine frequency, you don't just hear harmony; you become it.

My Story of Sound and Instant Transformation I remember a time when my husband and I had a disagreement at a festival featuring some of the top spiritual teachers and sound healers in the world. Feeling heavy from our argument, I entered a sound healing session, silently praying for peace.

By the end of the session, something remarkable happened. Every trace of frustration in my body had vanished. Instead, I felt an overwhelming joy and lightness. I ran into my husband's arms, hugging him tightly, and tears streamed down my face, not from pain or anger, but from pure love and gratitude. In that moment, I didn't even remember what we had argued about; all that remained was the deep, unconditional love I held for him and the profound appreciation for having him in my life.

This shift was instantaneous and unforgettable. Sound had bypassed the mind entirely and reset my energy, demonstrating in the most tangible way that vibration can heal, harmonize, and elevate our consciousness in real time.

Sacred Water Ritual

Water is the womb of the world. It is our first home and our constant companion. Every cell in our body carries its memory. The Sacred Water Ritual is a ceremony of purification, presence, and prayer—a way to reconnect with the flow of life through the simplest, most abundant element on earth.

From a scientific perspective, immersion and interaction with water—whether through bathing, showering, or natural bodies of water—has profound physiological effects. Research shows that hydrotherapy and water immersion can reduce stress hormone levels, regulate blood pressure, and enhance parasympathetic activity, bringing the body into deep rest and repair (Kakigi & Okada, 2024).

Warm water relaxes muscles and promotes emotional release, while cool water stimulates circulation and clarity. Spiritually, water is consciousness. It absorbs emotion, carries vibration, and responds to intention, mirroring our inner state back to us in ripples, reflections, and rhythm.

You don't need a luxurious bath or oceanside sanctuary to experience the sacred.

Even the water flowing from your home shower can become a channel for healing when you approach it with mindfulness.

Step 1: Set Your Intention Before turning on the water, pause. Place a hand on your heart and ask, "What do I need to cleanse, release, or call in today?" This simple act transforms routine into ritual.

Step 2: Prepare the Space For a bath, add Epsom salts, fresh herbs, or essential oils such as lavender, rosemary, or eucalyptus. For a shower, hang a small bundle of herbs from your shower head, add a few drops of oil to the corner of your shower, or light a candle nearby.

Sustainability begins with consciousness; use only the water you need, moving with gratitude and awareness of this shared resource.

Step 3: Enter the Flow As the water touches your skin, imagine it as liquid light washing away tension, fatigue, and stagnant energy. Visualize clarity flowing in with every drop. Inhale deeply. Exhale fully. Feel your nervous system soften as your energy realigns.

For deeper release, alternate between warm and cool water. This stimulates circulation, awakens the lymphatic system, and balances the body's energetic field.

Step 4: Speak to the Water Whisper your gratitude: "Sacred water, thank you for cleansing me, restoring me, and returning me to flow."

The vibration of your voice imprints into the water's molecular structure, a concept supported by emerging studies in cymatics and resonance.

Step 5: Seal the Ritual When you're finished, let the final stream of water run down your crown as you breathe in renewal. Step out slowly and pat your body dry, acknowledging the peace that now surrounds you.

This ritual unites the science of hydrotherapy with the soul of surrender.

Whether in a sacred bath or a mindful shower, you are participating in an ancient communion: cleansing the body, calming the mind, and remembering that you, too, are made of water.

Choose what resonates. Rotate rituals with seasons, moon phases, or inner needs. Alignment matters more than perfection. Spirit is always there, available, and waiting.

Water, My Sanctuary I don't remember the first time I realized how powerful water was, but I do remember when I first started making it a ritual. It was during college at Wichita State. I was overwhelmed, balancing life as a student-athlete, classes, and everything in between. I didn't even have a bathtub in my dorm room. One day, I asked a friend if I could use hers. I turned on "A Woman's Work" by Maxwell, sank into the warm water, and felt my worries dissolve with every moment.

> *"When you choose alignment over achievement, your life becomes a living prayer—guided, graceful, and grounded in truth—and you achieve everything in alignment with that truth."*

I had no idea why it worked (scientifically or spiritually) I only knew how I felt. That was the first time I experienced the profound effects of water: the tension leaving my body, the clarity entering my mind, the sense of peace settling in my soul. Since then, water has become my sanctuary. My showers, baths, and even moments in lakes or oceans are now sacred spaces where I reconnect with myself and with Spirit.

Closing Blessing

You don't have to do it all. You don't have to do it perfectly. Healing arrives in daily choices, whispered prayers, trusted breaths, and moments of stillness.

You are already whole.
You are already held.
You are already home.

Optional Exploration: Nurturing Your Spiritual Connection

Life Visioning, Michael Bernard Beckwith. A spiritual road map to align with your soul's highest purpose through visualization, meditation, and conscious awareness.

Spiritual Hygiene, Iyanla Vanzant. Guides readers through practices to clear emotional clutter and maintain energetic balance for spiritual renewal.

Homecoming, Dr. Thema Bryant. Teaches emotional restoration and self-compassion through reconnecting with your authentic self after pain or disconnection.

Vibrate Higher Daily, Lalah Delia. Encourages intentional living by raising your energetic frequency through mindfulness, healing, and self-love.

The Four Agreements, Don Miguel Ruiz. Reveals four simple yet profound principles to achieve personal freedom and inner peace.

The Untethered Soul, Michael A. Singer. Explores how to release limiting thoughts and emotional patterns to experience true spiritual liberation.

The Light Work, Jessica Zweig. A guide to authentic self-expression and empowered leadership rooted in self-worth and spiritual alignment.

These books are companions, not requirements. They shine a light on what's already within you.

References

Bratman, G. N., Daily, G. C., Levy, B. R., & Gross, J. J. (2019). Nature and mental health: An ecosystem service perspective. *Science Advances*, *5*(7), eaax0903. https://doi.org/10.1126/sciadv.aax0903.

Bratman, G. N., Hamilton, J. P., Hahn, K. S., Daily, G. C., & Gross, J. J. (2015). Nature experience reduces rumination and subgenual prefrontal cortex activation. *Proceedings of the National Academy of Sciences*, *12*(28), 8567–8572. 10.1073/pnas.1510459112.

Brown, R. P., & Gerbarg, P. L. (2005). Sudarshan Kriya yogic breathing in the treatment of stress, anxiety, and depression: Part I—neurophysiologic model. *Journal of Alternative and Complementary Medicine*, *11*(1), 189–201. 10.1089/acm.2005.11.189.

Driskell, J. E., Copper, C., & Moran, A. (1994). Does mental practice enhance performance? *Journal of Applied Psychology*, *79*(4), 481–492. 10.1037/0021-9010.79.4.481.

Emmons, R. A., & McCullough, M. E. (2003). Counting blessings versus burdens: An experimental investigation of gratitude and subjective well-being in daily life. *Journal of Personality and Social Psychology*, *84*(2), 377–389.

Kakigi, R., & Okada, K. (2024). Balneotherapy and cortisol levels: An updated systematic review and meta-analysis. *International Journal of Biometeorology*, *68*(10), 1909–1922. https://pubmed.ncbi.nlm.nih.gov/38884799/.

Lehrer, P. M., & Gevirtz, R. (2014). Heart rate variability biofeedback: How and why does it work? *Frontiers in Psychology*, *5*, 756. 10.3389/fpsyg.2014.00756.

Pew Research Center. (2017). Religion and well-being. https://www.pewresearch.org/religion/2017/01/12/religion-and-well-being/.

Yaden, D. B., Batz-Barbarich, C. L., Ng, V., Vaziri, H., Gladstone, J. N., Pawelski, J. O., & Tay, L. (2022). A meta-analysis of religion/spirituality and life satisfaction. *Journal of Happiness Studies*, *23*(8), 4147–4163. doi:10.1007/s10902-022-00558-7.

2 Emotional Wellbeing

Tohamina / Freepik

Your Emotions Aren't Your Enemy, They're Your Best Friend

There comes a moment when you realize your emotions are not your enemy; they are the language of your soul asking to be heard.

Emotional wellbeing is often misunderstood. For generations, society has conditioned us to hide, silence, or even fear our emotions. We've been told that showing anger makes us "difficult," expressing sadness makes us "weak," and revealing frustration makes us "ungrateful." Many of us learned to smile through pain, suppress our tears, and "stay positive" even when our hearts were breaking.

But the truth is this: Your emotions are not your enemy. They are not a sign that something is wrong with you. Your emotions are your deepest allies. They are sacred messengers bringing you truth. They are the language of your soul trying to express. They are the *true* compass of your inner world. When you learn to listen, honor, and embrace them, your emotions will guide you toward profound healing, spiritual awakening, and the fullness of who you're meant to be.

The Spiritual Purpose of Emotions

At the deepest level, emotions are energy in motion. They're vibrations that move through the body, arising to communicate something important about your experience. Spiritual traditions across the world, from ancient yogic philosophy to indigenous wisdom, teach us that emotions are portals into self-awareness. They show us where we are aligned with love and truth and, where we may still be holding onto fear, resistance, or pain.

Think of emotions as your soul's feedback system. Joy tells you what is nourishing your spirit. Sadness shows you where there is loss or longing. Anger reveals boundaries that have been crossed or values that have been dishonored. Fear alerts you to potential danger, but it also invites you to examine where you might be holding yourself back from growth.

When you view emotions through this spiritual lens, you begin to see them not as burdens to carry or battles to fight, but as teachers. Each one is a doorway into deeper awareness, compassion, and transformation.

The Science of Emotions

Modern science beautifully complements this spiritual wisdom. Neuroscience tells us that emotions are not random; they are biological signals designed to help us survive and thrive. They arise from complex interactions with the brain, body, and nervous system.

For example:

- The amygdala in the brain acts like an emotional radar, detecting threats and triggering fear or anger to protect you.
- The prefrontal cortex helps regulate and interpret emotions, giving you the ability to reflect, choose, and grow.
- The vagus nerve, which runs from the brain to the gut, connects your emotions to your physical state, influencing heart rate, digestion, and even immune response. This is why stress can upset your stomach or why calmness can slow your heartbeat.

Emotions are also deeply connected to neurotransmitters and hormones; serotonin, dopamine, oxytocin, and cortisol all rise and fall depending on what you feel. Research in psychoneuroimmunology even shows that repressed emotions can weaken the immune system, while authentic emotional expression supports resilience and health.

In other words, when you suppress your emotions, you're not avoiding them, you're storing them in your body. Over time, unprocessed emotions can manifest as tension, chronic stress, or even illness. But when you allow emotions to flow, you restore harmony to your nervous system and create conditions for healing at every level.

Why We Fear Our Emotions

Despite this wisdom, many of us still see emotions as threats. Why? Because we live in a culture that glorifies control and productivity over presence and authenticity. We are taught to "push through," "get over it," or "keep it together."

But here's the paradox: The more we resist emotions, the more power they gain over us. Suppressed emotions don't disappear; they linger in the subconscious, shaping our behavior and choices. They can erupt unexpectedly as rage, anxiety, or deep sadness. Or they can quietly drain us, leaving us disconnected from joy and aliveness.

When we embrace emotions instead of fearing them, they lose their grip. Anger, when honored, becomes a force for justice and clarity. Sadness, when expressed, opens the heart to compassion. Even fear, when faced with courage, becomes a teacher of trust and surrender.

Emotions as Pathways to Healing

Healing does not come from avoiding pain, but from moving through it. Emotions are the path. They point to wounds that need nurturing, stories that need rewriting, and parts of yourself that are longing to be seen.

For example, when grief arises after a loss, it is not trying to break you, it is helping you process love that no longer has a physical outlet. When anger rises in the face of injustice, it is not "negative," it is your body's way of saying, this is not in alignment with truth. When joy bubbles up unexpectedly, it's your soul reminding you that life is still worth celebrating, no matter what you've been through.

From a therapeutic perspective, psychologists like Dr. Bessel van der Kolk (author of *The Body Keeps the Score*) show that trauma and suppressed emotions live in the body. Healing requires more than thinking your way out; it requires feeling your way through. Breathwork, movement, meditation, and somatic practices are powerful tools to release stored emotional energy and restore wholeness.

Practical Steps to Befriend Your Emotions

1. **Pause and breathe:** When a strong emotion arises, instead of reacting immediately, pause. Take a few deep breaths. This activates the parasympathetic nervous system, helping you shift from reactivity to awareness.
2. **Name the emotion:** Neuroscience shows that labeling emotions by simply saying "I feel angry" or "I feel sad" calms the amygdala and activates the prefrontal cortex, giving you more clarity and choice.
3. **Feel it in the body:** Ask yourself, "Where do I feel this emotion?" Maybe anger feels like heat in the chest or sadness feels like heaviness in the shoulders. Notice without judgment.
4. **Honor the message:** Every emotion carries wisdom. Ask, "What is this feeling trying to tell me? What needs attention, healing, or change?"
5. **Express safely:** Emotions need expression. Journal, dance, cry, scream into a pillow, paint, pray; find ways to let the energy move through you rather than get stuck inside.
6. **Seek support:** Sometimes emotions feel too big to hold alone. Therapy, coaching, or community support can provide the safe container you need to process and transform them.

The Gift of Emotional Wholeness

When you stop fighting your emotions and start listening to them, life changes. You move from being a prisoner of suppressed feelings to being a conscious cocreator with them. Emotional wellbeing does not mean being happy all the time; it means being authentic, expressive, and alive.

You begin to see emotions not as storms to fear but as waves to ride. Some waves are gentle, others are intense, but all are part of the ocean of your being. The more you allow them to flow, the more connected you feel to yourself, to others, and to God.

Spiritual teachers remind us that emotions are sacred portals. They dissolve the illusion of separation and reconnect us to the truth of our humanity. And science confirms that when we embrace emotions, we unlock resilience, health, and vitality.

So the next time you feel anger, sadness, fear, or joy, remember that this is not your enemy. This is your friend. This is your soul speaking. This is life moving through you.

Your emotions are not mistakes to be fixed, nor obstacles to your spiritual path. They *are* the path. They are the whispers of your heart, the intelligence of your body, and the wisdom of your spirit.

When you embrace them, you embrace yourself. When you trust them, you trust life. And when you honor them, you step into the fullness of your divine wholeness.

Emotional wellbeing begins with one radical truth: Your emotions are your best friends.

> *"Emotional wellbeing begins when you give yourself permission to feel fully, without apology, without shame, and without rushing the process."*

My Story: Befriending My Anger

I'll never forget a particular evening that shifted the way I related to my emotions forever. It started with what seemed like a simple, yet difficult, conversation with a loved one. Words were exchanged, but beneath the words lived something deeper: an ache, a longing, and an unspoken wound. As the conversation ended, I felt a wave of heat rise through my body. My chest tightened, my jaw clenched, and I recognized the familiar fire of anger.

In the past, I would have done what many of us are taught to do: swallow it down, plaster on a smile, and tell myself to "get over it." Or I would have gone to the opposite extreme: letting it spill out in ways that only caused more disconnection and pain. But that night, something in me whispered, "Pause."

So I did.

I sat quietly, hands resting on my lap, feeling the fire surge inside. And instead of pushing it away, I turned inward and asked softly, almost as if speaking to a child, "What are you trying to tell me?"

At first, there was just silence. The raw heat of anger pulsed in my body, uncomfortable and insistent. But as I stayed with it—breathing, allowing, listening—something surprising happened. Beneath the fire was a clear voice, a simple but profound truth; my heart was asking for respect. Respect for myself, respect for the other person, and respect for the sacredness of our relationship.

That moment became a turning point.

Anger as a Messenger

Up until then, I had always seen anger as a "bad" emotion, something dangerous, shameful, or destructive. Society reinforces this belief constantly. We're told to "be nice," "stay calm," and "not make a scene." Women especially are conditioned to suppress anger because it doesn't align with the role of being agreeable, accommodating, or "spiritual."

But sitting with my anger that night, I realized it wasn't there to destroy me. It wasn't there to burn bridges or create chaos. It was there to protect me. To guide me. To tell me that something I valued deeply—mutual respect—was out of balance.

This was the first time I experienced anger not as an enemy but as a messenger.

Everyday Lessons in Listening

That realization didn't just change the way I approached big, emotional conversations; it transformed the way I showed up in everyday life.

Like in traffic, for example. Like many people, I used to feel my blood pressure rise the second someone cut me off. I'd grip the steering wheel tighter, replaying the "injustice" in my mind. But when I began treating anger as a friend, I started asking, "What are you trying to show me here?"

Often, it wasn't really about the other driver. It was about my relationship to control. Traffic taught me patience, surrender, and the truth that I can't control others, only how I respond.

The same lesson showed up at work. A client dismissed my ideas in a meeting, and the feeling of frustration was immediate. Before, I might have stuffed it down, telling myself not to take it personally. But by listening, I realized frustration was pointing me toward self-advocacy. I spoke up calmly and assertively; instead of creating conflict, it actually earned me more respect. Once I was able to articulate and demonstrate my perspective. They absolutely loved it.

Even at home, in the small, everyday moments—like repeating the same request to my husband for the third time. I learned that frustration was my signal to pause and ask, "What boundary needs to be set? What expectation needs to be clarified?" These simple shifts not only brought me more peace but they also deepened my relationships.

Learning to Sit with My Emotions

From that night forward, I began practicing a new way of relating to all my emotions. Instead of immediately judging them as "good" or "bad," I started sitting with them, listening without rushing to fix, suppress, or express them in harmful ways.

It wasn't easy at first. Emotions can feel overwhelming, like tidal waves threatening to sweep us under. Fear whispers, "If you let this out, it will never stop." Shame adds, "People will think less of you if they see this side of you." But the more I practiced, the more I discovered that emotions, when met with compassion, have a natural rhythm. They rise, peak, and fall—like waves in the ocean.

The real danger isn't in feeling them. The danger is in resisting them. Suppressed emotions don't vanish. They linger in the body as tension, stress, or even illness. They show up in relationships as resentment or withdrawal. They surface in unexpected moments, often with more force than if we had honored them in the first place.

By learning to sit with my emotions, I began to unlock their wisdom. Anger taught me about boundaries. Sadness revealed where I was still grieving losses I hadn't acknowledged. Fear showed me where I was playing small, holding back from growth. And joy reminded me that presence, not perfection, was the key to fulfillment.

Transformation in Relationships

This practice of listening changed not only my inner world but also my outer world, especially my relationships.

When I started acknowledging my emotions instead of burying them, my communication shifted. Instead of lashing out in anger, I could calmly express, "I feel disrespected when this happens, and I need us to create a different dynamic." Instead of hiding sadness, I could vulnerably share, "I'm hurting right now, and I need support."

The result? Many of my relationships deepened. The very feelings I once feared became the gateway to greater intimacy, trust, and authenticity.

At the same time, I learned that not everyone will respond the way I hoped. Some people may resist hearing your true emotions or may not be ready to change. Accepting this reality became part of the practice. I learned to hold my boundaries, release expectations, and focus on the connections where mutual respect and understanding were possible.

Strengthening Self-Respect

The greatest gift of this journey has been the growth of self-respect. When you honor your emotions, you're essentially saying to yourself, "I matter. My inner experience matters. My truth deserves to be heard."

For years, I had unknowingly dismissed my own needs in the name of harmony, productivity, or image. But by befriending my emotions, I started reclaiming my voice and my worth. I realized that respecting myself wasn't selfish, it was the foundation for living authentically and loving others more fully.

Self-respect became a sacred practice. Each time I listened to my emotions, I was building trust with myself. I was telling my inner child, my soul, my body, "I will not abandon you." And with that trust came a deeper sense of peace, confidence, and wholeness.

Every Emotion as a Doorway

Through this journey, I've come to see every emotion as a doorway:

- Joy opens the door to gratitude and celebration.
- Anger opens the door to boundaries and justice.

- Sadness opens the door to compassion and healing.
- Fear opens the door to courage and growth.
- Grief opens the door to love's depth and the power of letting go.

Each doorway leads to deeper self-knowledge, and, ultimately, deeper freedom.

A New Way of Seeing

Looking back, I realize that what once felt like a battlefield (my emotional landscape) has now become a compass pointing me toward alignment with my highest self.

Do I still feel anger? Absolutely. Do I still feel fear, sadness, or doubt? Of course. But now, instead of fighting them, I greet them with curiosity. "What wisdom do you carry? What are you asking me to see?"

This shift has changed everything. It has given me permission to be fully human: messy, complex, radiant, and nuanced. And it has shown me that emotions are not obstacles on the spiritual path. They are the path.

My story began with one simple moment: sitting with anger instead of running from it. What unfolded was not just healing but transformation. Relationships blossomed. Self-respect grew. Emotional intelligence strengthened. And a new way of living emerged—one rooted in authenticity, compassion, and presence.

If there's one thing I hope you take from my story, it's this: Your emotions are not your enemy. They are your best friends. They are your teachers, your protectors, and your guides. When you listen, they will always lead you back home—to yourself, to love, and to the truth of who you really are.

> *"True healing begins the moment you allow yourself to feel without judgment, knowing that every tear, every laugh, every silence has wisdom in it."*

Why Emotional Wellbeing Matters

Scientific research supports what ancient wisdom has long taught: Emotions are not distractions, they are vital signals for mental, physical, and spiritual health. They are the bridge between your inner and outer world, between your biology and your soul.

The Benefits of Emotional Awareness

Embracing emotional awareness, however, transforms your relationship with yourself and the world around you. Research has shown that emotional awareness can do the following:

- **Boost resilience and regulate stress hormones:** Recognizing and processing emotions allows the nervous system to reset, preventing chronic activation of fight-or-flight responses (Kashdan & Rottenberg, 2010).
- **Reduce emotional reactivity and promote clarity:** Naming and understanding emotions decreases impulsive responses and increases thoughtful decision-making (Chambers et al., 2009).
- **Improve mood and cognitive function through creative expression:** Engaging with emotions in productive ways—such as journaling, art, or movement—stimulates the brain, improves focus, and enhances problem-solving (Stuckey & Nobel, 2010).

In practical terms, emotional awareness enables you to respond to life from a place of choice rather than reaction. It builds self-confidence, strengthens relationships, and nurtures a sense of inner calm despite challenges.

Suppressing emotions, however, increases the risk of anxiety, depression, chronic illness, and disconnection from your authentic self. Emotional wellbeing is not a luxury; it's a survival skill and a spiritual practice.

The Invitation: Befriend Your Emotions

Imagine emotions as wise companions walking beside you. Anger whispers, "Protect your boundaries." Sadness says, "Something precious was lost." Joy sings, "This is where you come alive." Fear murmurs, "Look carefully before you leap."

The shift happens when you stop resisting and start listening. Your emotions are not interruptions; they are invitations.

Daily Ritual: Emotional Awareness Practice

1. **Pause and breathe:** When a strong emotion arises, place your hand on your heart or belly. Breathe deeply, three times. Feel your body soften.

2. **Name the emotion:** "I feel sadness." "I feel anger." Naming calms the nervous system and brings clarity.
3. **Dialogue with the emotion:** Ask, "What are you here to show me?" Listen without judgment.
4. **Anchor the wisdom:** Journal the insights or speak them aloud. Affirm, "Thank you, my friend, for showing me what matters most."

Over time, this daily practice builds inner trust. Your emotions stop feeling like floods and begin to feel like rivers you can navigate with grace.

A Client Story: The Breakthrough Session

When she first walked into the room, her energy told the story before her words did. Shoulders slightly hunched, eyes darting down, she carried the heaviness of someone who had been holding it all together for far too long. She had learned to smile when she wanted to cry, to say "I'm fine" when her inner world was begging to be seen. What drew her here wasn't just curiosity; it was exhaustion. She was tired of carrying the invisible weight of emotions she didn't understand and couldn't release.

In our initial conversation, she confessed that she had always been the strong one—the caretaker, the achiever, the one everyone leaned on in moments of crisis. But she no longer knew how to lean on herself. She felt numb and disconnected, yet simmering underneath was a volcano of unexpressed emotions: anger she wasn't allowed to show, grief tucked away, and shame buried under perfectionism.

I guided her to lie down, reminding her that this was a safe space. All she had to do was breathe.

The breathwork began gently: inhales expanding her chest, exhales softening her belly. At first, her breaths were shallow, controlled, almost apologetic. With encouragement and reminders that she was safe, her chest rose higher, exhalations grew louder, and her body remembered what it meant to surrender.

(*continued*)

(continued)

Within minutes, release began. Tears fell slowly at first, then with increasing intensity. A deep, primal scream followed, tearing through the silence of the room. It wasn't just noise, it was truth: rage, grief, and power that had been caged inside her body for years. Her fists unclenched, her body trembled and softened, moving among crying, screaming, and silence. Waves of energy coursed through her, as if her nervous system were finally unclogging from years of repression. I stayed beside her, holding space without judgment.

When her body began to still, I placed a journal beside her and invited her to write down what she was feeling. Her hand shook as she wrote, but the words came quickly: raw, unfiltered, unedited. Page after page captured what had never been voiced. Words like, "I'm tired of pretending," "I'm angry I wasn't protected," and "I want to be free" gave her feelings a home. Reading them aloud, she felt permission to release, to exist fully in her own experience.

Then she lay back with a long, shuddering exhale, as though even her breath was relieved that the truth was finally on paper. I played sound bowls to balance her energy centers and ground her energy. The room felt lighter. Her shoulders began to open, her chest lifted, and her eyes, red from crying, glowed with a softness that hadn't been there when she arrived. She whispered, "I feel . . . free," and then laughed: a full, deep laugh that carried the sound of release, of lightness, of a woman letting go of a thousand invisible pounds.

A note on the process: While some shifts happened during this session, emotional release is often a process that unfolds over days, weeks, or months. Each person's journey is unique, and some experiences require multiple sessions to reach similar breakthroughs. What matters most is the presence, the willingness to feel, and the courage to listen to your emotions.

Over the next few days, she reported feeling lighter, with more energy and less tension in her body. Conversations with family felt easier because she no longer carried the same resentment in her chest.

The volcano inside her had not disappeared; it had transformed. What once felt like an eruption waiting to happen had become a steady, warm, life-giving fire.

This is the power of emotional release. Emotions, when denied, burrow into the body, manifesting as muscle tension, shallow breaths, racing thoughts, or restless nights. When given space, they reveal themselves as allies. Each tear is a teacher, each scream a boundary, each journaled word a step toward freedom.

Her story is not an exception, it is a mirror. It reflects what is possible when we stop fearing our emotions and start listening to them. Healing isn't about perfection; it's about presence. And presence is exactly what she found when she walked out of that room.

Seven Emotional Wellbeing Rituals

Transformational Letter Writing Ritual

When emotions are bottled, they often resurface as stress, anxiety, or even physical pain. Writing gives them a voice. According to Pennebaker (1997), expressive writing has been shown to reduce trauma symptoms, boost immune function, and increase overall wellbeing. Spiritually, letter writing becomes a prayer in ink; it's your soul speaking through your hand.

A Client Story

One of my clients, Tiffany, struggled with unprocessed grief after her father's passing. She felt stuck: unable to move forward, yet afraid to let go. Through Transformational Letter Writing, she wrote a raw, tear-soaked letter beginning with, "Dear Dad . . . ." She poured out her regrets, love, and unanswered questions. When she closed the letter with a blessing; "May your soul rest in peace, and may I carry your love with grace" she felt something shift. Burning the letter became her sacred release. She later shared, "I finally feel like I'm breathing again."

How to Practice

1. Create a quiet space with pen, paper, and maybe a candle.
2. Begin with "Dear [Emotion, Person, or Situation]. . . ."
3. Write without censoring. Let the words flow raw and real.
4. Close with a blessing, prayer, or release statement.
5. Choose what to do with the letter: Keep it in a journal for integration or burn it as release.

Reflection Prompts

- What emotion most needs a voice today?
- What words remain unsaid, and how does it feel to release them?
- What blessing can I give myself in this moment?

> *"Emotional freedom comes when you stop resisting what you feel and start trusting that even your hardest emotions are leading you toward wholeness."*

Creative Expression Ritual

Emotions are energy in motion. When expressed through art, dance, music, or movement, they transform. By giving emotions a physical or visual outlet, we allow the body and mind to release tension, regulate mood, and process experiences more fully.

Creativity becomes a bridge between emotion and embodiment, enabling what is felt but unspoken to move through you safely. Spiritually, creativity is prayer made visible: Each movement, brushstroke, or beat becomes a way to witness, honor, and release what lives inside you.

Research supports this: Creative arts therapy has been shown to reduce stress, enhance cognitive function, and improve emotional regulation (Stuckey & Nobel, 2010).

A Client Story

Marcus came to me overwhelmed with anger after a difficult breakup. Traditional talk therapy left him feeling stuck in his head. I invited him into creative expression, through drumming.

At first, he resisted. "I'm not musical; it's just something I did as a kid." But soon, each beat became a release. His anger turned into rhythm, rhythm into flow. Afterward, he said, "For the first time in months, I don't feel heavy."

How to Practice

1. Pick your medium. Paint, dance, drumming, sculpting, singing, or any movement that resonates. Optional: Improvise with everyday objects—tap your desk, clap, or use household items as instruments.
2. Set an intention. Whisper or think, "I allow my emotions to move through me."
3. Express without aiming for beauty or perfection. Focus on process, not product.
4. Close your practice. Place your hand over your creation and say, "Thank you." This honors the energy you've released.

Reflection Prompts

- If my sadness had a color, what would it be?
- If my joy had a sound, how would it move through me?
- How does my body feel after creating?

"Every pause you take to breathe through a trigger, every boundary you set with love, every moment you choose compassion over reaction—that's emotional wellbeing in practice."

Soul Scribing Ritual (Conversations with Spirit)

Emotional storms can cloud clarity. Soul Scribing cuts through the fog. Neuroscience shows that writing activates brain networks involved in self-reflection, memory, and emotional processing, helping us access deeper insights through embodied expression (Marano et al., 2025). Spiritually, writing opens a channel for divine wisdom to meet human emotion.

A Client Story

Jasmine, a business owner, came to me paralyzed by fear during a career transition. Through Soul Scribing, she lit a candle, took a deep breath, and asked, "Spirit, what do I need to know right now?" Her pen began to write words she later described as "not my own but exactly what I needed." Phrases like "Trust the timing. You are guided" became her anchor.

How to Practice

1. Light a candle and breathe deeply.
2. Ask Spirit, "What truth do I need to hear?"
3. Write without judgment or editing.
4. Re-read later, highlighting wisdom that feels divinely inspired.

Reflection Prompts

- What wisdom came through that surprised me?
- How did I feel while writing—calm, tense, peaceful?
- Which words feel like mantras for me today?

"When you honor your emotions instead of hiding them, you don't just find balance, you find alignment with your deepest truth."

Neuro-Emotional Regulation Ritual (4-4-4 Breath)

Stress hijacks the nervous system, locking us in fight-or-flight. Conscious breath reclaims balance. Studies confirm that paced breathing stimulates the vagus nerve, lowering cortisol and calming the mind (Brown & Gerbarg, 2005).

A Client Story

During a corporate retreat, I taught the 4-4-4 breath to a group of executives drowning in stress. One participant, a CEO, later told me, "I went into a high-stakes meeting and instead of panicking, I used the breath. I led with a regulated nervous system for the first time in years."

How to Practice

1. Inhale deeply through your nose for four counts.
2. Hold gently for four counts.
3. Exhale slowly through your mouth for four counts.
4. Repeat for seven cycles, adding visualization of light on inhale, tension on exhale.

Reflection Prompts

- How does my body feel before and after this breathwork?
- What images arise as I visualize light and release?
- How can I use this tool in moments of stress?

Trigger Transformation Ritual

Triggers are not enemies; they are teachers pointing to unhealed places. Mindful processing rewires emotional responses (Siegel, 2012). Spiritually, a trigger is a sacred mirror.

A Client Story

Elena constantly clashed with her teenage daughter. Every argument left her feeling dismissed and enraged. Through the Trigger Transformation Ritual, she learned to pause, name the emotion ("I feel disrespected"), and trace it back to childhood wounds. With compassion, she whispered, "I forgive. I release. I choose peace." She later said, "Instead of fighting my daughter, I started healing my inner child."

How to Practice

1. Pause.
2. Name the emotion.
3. Trace its root.
4. Ask, "What is this teaching me?"
5. Release with compassion.

Reflection Prompts

- What emotions surface most often when I'm triggered?
- What childhood or past experiences connect to them?
- What compassion can I extend to myself?

Brain State Check-In Ritual

Our brains operate in states: survival (fight/flight), emotional (reactive), and executive (creative/calm). Awareness builds regulation. Davidson (2003) found that mindful brain awareness strengthens resilience.

> **A Client Story**
>
> Jordan, a busy entrepreneur, constantly made reactive decisions under stress. By setting hourly reminders to check his brain state, he caught himself spiraling. Using breath and grounding, he shifted into executive mode before making decisions. He shared, "For the first time, my choices feel aligned instead of panicked."

How to Practice

1. Set a reminder to pause each hour.
2. Ask, "Am I in survival, emotional, or executive brain?"
3. Use breathwork or grounding to shift into calm.

Reflection Prompts

- What brain state do I spend most of my day in?
- How do I feel when I shift into executive mode?
- What tools help me transition fastest?

Gratitude for Emotional Growth Ritual

Gratitude reframes emotions as allies. Emmons and McCullough (2003) found that gratitude increases resilience, optimism, and wellbeing. Spiritually, gratitude turns pain into purpose.

A Client Story

Sophia used to dread her anxiety attacks. Through this ritual, she began each evening by writing, "Thank you, anxiety, for reminding me to slow down. Thank you, joy, for showing me I am safe." Soon, her fear transformed into appreciation for the wisdom within her emotions.

How to Practice

1. Each evening, list emotions you felt.
2. For each, write what it taught you.
3. Speak them aloud or share with a partner.

Reflection Prompts

- What emotions visited me today, and what did they teach me?
- How does gratitude shift how I see "negative" emotions?
- Which emotions feel like unexpected allies?

Client Story: Healing Across a Screen

She almost didn't book the session.

The idea of doing deep emotional work over Zoom felt strange to her. Healing, she thought, needed to happen in person; eye to eye, breath to breath, body to body. But life circumstances made travel impossible and something in her heart whispered to give it a try. With a mixture of curiosity and skepticism, she clicked the link and entered the virtual room.

The moment her face appeared on screen, I could feel her energy. Her smile was polite but tight, her posture held with the kind of stiffness that betrays inner turmoil. She admitted right away, "I don't know if this is going to work. I feel so disconnected from myself and, honestly, from everyone." It was the disconnection that brought her here—not just from people, but from her own emotions, her joy, her body.

(*continued*)

(continued)

We began with grounding. I asked her to place her hand on her heart, close her eyes, and breathe. She hesitated at first, keeping her breaths shallow, her mind racing with doubt. But slowly, the rhythm of intentional breathing began to soften the edges of her resistance. I reminded her: The energy we access in healing is not limited by space or time. Connection is not about proximity; it is about presence.

As the breathwork deepened, her face softened. Her breaths grew audible, her chest rising and falling in waves. Then came the shaking. At first just her hands trembled, then her shoulders, then her whole body quivered as though decades of unspoken words were vibrating out of her cells. I guided her to let the energy move, to trust what was happening, to allow without trying to control.

That was when the tears came. Silent at first, then spilling freely down her cheeks. "I don't even know why I'm crying," she whispered. But she didn't need to know. The body knew. The body always remembers what the mind forgets.

I invited her to journal between breaths, to give the emotions words. She scribbled furiously, her pen barely keeping up with the flood of thoughts. Phrases emerged: "I feel like I've been wearing a mask for years." "I don't recognize myself anymore." "I want to feel alive again." She looked up at the screen, eyes wet, voice trembling. "I didn't realize how numb I had been until now."

We shifted into movement. I played a song with a slow, grounding rhythm and asked her to let her body respond. At first, she swayed cautiously in her chair. I invited her to stand and listen to her body; she stood, letting her arms move in wide circles, letting her hips sway, letting her body remember freedom. And then, almost out of nowhere, she laughed. A full, unexpected laugh that filled the room on both sides of the screen.

"Why am I laughing?" she asked through tears.

"Because laughter is a release," I reminded her. "Because your body is remembering joy."

The session unfolded like waves; crying, laughing, writing, breathing. She experienced in one hour what she hadn't felt in years: aliveness. Connection. The truth of her emotions moving freely through her instead of being locked inside.

As we closed, she sat down, her face glowing with a softness that hadn't been there when we began. She said quietly, "I can't believe this happened over Zoom. I actually feel . . . connected. To myself. To you. To life."

In the days that followed, she emailed me updates. She described feeling lighter, more energized, more compassionate toward herself. She had begun journaling daily, creating space for her emotions instead of burying them. She started moving her body more—sometimes dancing in her kitchen, sometimes just stretching and breathing with awareness. What surprised her most wasn't just the emotional release, but the spiritual clarity that came with it. She described feeling guided again, as though she had tuned back into the frequency of her own soul.

This is the beauty of emotional healing: It is not confined to a location, a building, or a specific practice. It is not limited by technology or distance. True healing flows through intention, presence, and willingness. When someone shows up fully, even in a square on a screen, the energy has space to move. And when energy moves, transformation follows.

Her story is proof that emotions are not bound by time or place. They are living energy, waiting for us to pay attention. They don't require perfect conditions; they require permission. Permission to cry. Permission to shake. Permission to laugh. Permission to feel.

What she discovered in that session, and what many discover when they dare to open themselves to this work, is that emotional wellbeing is not about circumstances. It is about connection. It is about choosing presence, even through a laptop camera. It is about remembering that your emotions are not flaws in your system, but signals from your soul, guiding you home.

And sometimes, home is only a breath away.

Final Blessing

May you befriend your emotions instead of fearing them.

May anger become your protector, sadness your healer, joy your compass, fear your teacher.

> *"The most sacred journey of emotional wellbeing is not about becoming unshakable, but about learning to bend, release, and rise stronger every single time."*

May every feeling remind you that you are alive, growing, and guided.

You are not broken—you are beautifully whole.

Optional Exploration: Caring for Your Emotional Wellbeing

The Body Keeps the Score, Bessel van der Kolk, MD. Explains how trauma reshapes the body and mind and offers paths to healing through somatic and emotional awareness.

The Garden Within, Dr. Anita Phillips. Invites you to see emotions not as obstacles but as fertile ground for healing and emotional strength, rooted in both science and lived experience.

Atlas of the Heart, Brené Brown. Maps the full range of human emotions to help cultivate language, empathy, and meaningful connection.

More Than Enough, Elaine Welteroth. A memoir of self-discovery and emotional empowerment, inspiring readers to own their worth and purpose.

The Emotional Life of Your Brain, Richard J. Davidson and Sharon Begley. Explores how different emotional styles shape our lives and how to cultivate resilience and happiness.

Finding Me, Viola Davis. An unflinchingly honest memoir of healing, courage, and self-acceptance through vulnerability and authenticity.

How Are You, Really?, Jenna Kutcher. Encourages deep self-reflection and emotional honesty to create a life aligned with your true desires.

These books are companions on your emotional journey. Some offer daily exercises, others share stories or memoir, and some include research-backed strategies. Open to them when you feel drawn, and let your intuition guide which messages resonate most deeply.

Remember: Your emotional wisdom is already within you. These resources simply help you access, honor, and integrate it more fully.

References

Brown, R. P., & Gerbarg, P. L. (2005). Sudarshan Kriya yogic breathing in the treatment of stress, anxiety, and depression. *Journal of Alternative and Complementary Medicine, 11*(4), 711–717.

Chambers, R., Gullone, E., & Allen, N. B. (2009). Mindful emotion regulation: An integrative review. *Clinical Psychology Review, 29*(6), 560–572.

Davidson, R. J. (2003). Affective neuroscience and psychophysiology: Toward a synthesis. *Psychophysiology, 40*(5), 655–665.

Emmons, R. A., & McCullough, M. E. (2003). Counting blessings versus burdens: An experimental investigation of gratitude and subjective well-being in daily life. *Journal of Personality and Social Psychology, 84*(2), 377–389.

Kashdan, T. B., & Rottenberg, J. (2010). Psychological flexibility as a fundamental aspect of health. *Clinical Psychology Review, 30*(7), 865–878.

Marano, G., Kotzalidis, G. D., Lisci, F. M., Anesini, M. B., Rossi, S., Barbonetti, S., Cangini, A., Ronsisvalle, A., Artuso, L., Falsini, C., & Caso, R. (2025). The neuroscience behind writing: Handwriting vs. typing—who wins the battle?" *Life (Basel), 15*(3), 345.

Pennebaker, J. W. (1997). Writing about emotional experiences as a therapeutic process. *Psychological Science, 8*(3), 162–166.

Siegel, D. J. (2012). *The developing mind: How relationships and the brain interact to shape who we are* (2nd ed.) Guilford Press.

Stuckey, H. L., & Nobel, J. (2010). The connection between art, healing, and public health. *American Journal of Public Health, 100*(2), 254–263.

3 Mental Wellbeing

Tohamina / Freepik

The Sacred Practice of Resilience

There comes a moment when you realize your mind is not who you are; it is only the narrator, not the author of your life.

Mental wellbeing is not a luxury; it's a sacred practice, a daily ritual of tending to your mind like you would care for a garden or a child. Every thought, every pause, every breath is an opportunity to cultivate clarity, creativity, and inner peace. In this chapter, you are invited to explore the Sacred NeuroReset Method, my spiritually grounded framework for training the mind and rewiring neural pathways. Through Awakening, Permission, Healing, Trust, Practice, Alignment, and Transformation, you will learn to observe your thoughts, release limiting patterns, cultivate resilience, and align your energy with your soul's intentions.

But before the rituals, I want to take you deeper into the personal experiences that shaped my relationship with my mind—the moments that taught me that my thoughts were narrators, not dictators, and that mental freedom is cultivated, not inherited.

Awakening—Your Mind Is Not Who You Are

I first encountered awakening as a child living in a small trailer with my mom, dad, two brothers, and my younger sister. Our space was tight. Our clothes often came from charity donations. Luxuries (ice cream on a summer afternoon, a brand-new pair of shoes) were rare and fleeting. But even within that scarcity, my imagination thrived.

After a rainstorm, I would rush outside, mud oozing between my toes, and create mud pies with complete joy. I would smear wet earth across flat stones, stacking and sculpting, pretending I was running a bakery. At the time, I was too young to cook, too small to plant a garden, but in that mud, I was practicing creation. Each piece of mud was a tiny act of creating my vision for my future.

Even the gray, overcast skies above our trailer seemed to invite my imagination. I remember sitting on the steps, watching puddles reflect the clouds, and hearing my mind whisper, "This is all there is. This is your life." But even as that voice echoed, I would imagine walking on sunny beaches in far-off countries, exploring cities I had only glimpsed on TV, feeling the warmth of the sun and the rhythm of new streets beneath my feet.

Those daydreams were my first lessons in mental freedom. My mind could narrate fear, scarcity, and limitation, but it could also narrate hope, creativity, and possibility. Even as a child, I had a choice: I could let my circumstances define me, or I could step into the story I wanted to live.

> *"Mental awakening begins the moment you realize your thoughts are not your truth; they are merely the storyteller."*

Early Lessons in Resilience and Creation

Growing up, I learned quickly that life could be unpredictable. One week we might have enough to fill our stomachs, and the next week we would stretch each remaining dollar as far as possible. I learned to read my parents' moods, anticipate what we might need, and find joy in small victories. But while these practical skills were essential for survival, it was my imagination that gave me resilience.

Books, television, and simple observations of the world became portals to other realities. I was an avid viewer of documentaries and travel shows, I would watch people cooking in Paris, walking the streets of Tokyo, or surfing in Brazil. I would replay these moments in my mind until I felt as if I had traveled there myself. These were not just fantasies; they were exercises in mental rehearsal, a concept I later read about in the work of Joe Dispenza in *Breaking the Habit of Being Yourself.* I was unconsciously training my brain to expand beyond the limitations of my environment.

Even the smallest creative acts—sketching, rearranging my simple belongings, writing stories in my journal—taught me that the mind could shape reality. Norman Doidge's (2007) *The Brain That Changes Itself* would later confirm what I had felt intuitively: The brain is malleable, capable of forming new neural pathways when challenged, engaged, and nurtured. My early play and daydreaming were the seeds of what would become a lifelong practice of mental rewiring through awareness, visualization, and intentional thought.

Lessons from Presence and Awareness

As I grew older, I began to notice the patterns of my thoughts. Anxiety, self-doubt, and fear of not having enough were common narrators in my mind, just as hope, curiosity, and creativity were. I learned that noticing these patterns was the first step toward reclaiming agency over them.

Eckhart Tolle's (1997) *The Power of Now* taught me that the present moment is the only place where true mental freedom exists. Looking back, my childhood mud pies and puddle reflections were exercises in presence. I was fully engaged in the moment—hands covered in wet earth, body moving with joy, mind alive in the now. These moments were early encounters with what Mihaly Csikszentmihalyi (1990) calls *flow*: a state of total immersion and engagement that transcends fear and limitation. Flow doesn't require wealth, comfort, or privilege; it only requires presence and attention.

Vex King's (2018) *Good Vibes, Good Life* later gave me language for what I felt intuitively: Cultivating the mind through positivity, gratitude, and conscious intention is not superficial—it is a spiritual practice. Even as a child, my imagination, my curiosity, and my daydreams were acts of raising vibration, training my mind to focus on possibility rather than limitation.

Permission to Expand Beyond Circumstances

One of the most profound lessons from my early life was that permission is key. Permission to dream, to create, to imagine a different story for yourself, even when the world around you tells you otherwise.

I remember a moment when my mother, exhausted after a long day at work, handed me a notebook and said, "Write down whatever you want to do when you grow up. Don't let anyone tell you what you can't." That simple act, a small gesture in the chaos of our day-to-day survival, was revolutionary. It was the first time I felt I had explicit permission to shape my mind and my life.

Carol Dweck's (2006) *Mindset* later articulated what I was beginning to understand instinctively: Growth and possibility are not fixed; they are cultivated. My early exercises in creativity, imagination, and self-directed play were, in essence, practice in building a growth mindset. I was learning, even in a tiny trailer, that the stories my mind told were flexible, and I had the power to rewrite them.

Emotional Intelligence and Connection

Even as a child, I felt the invisible currents of emotional energy around me; the tension in my parents' voices, the unspoken worries of my siblings, the quiet hope that everything would somehow be okay. Learning to notice these subtleties taught me empathy, resilience, and emotional literacy, even before I knew those were formal concepts.

Brené Brown's *Atlas of the Heart* (2021) and Susan David's (2016) *Emotional Agility* later gave me vocabulary and strategies to refine what I had begun to practice instinctively. Observing my mind, naming my feelings, and responding rather than reacting became foundational practices for mental wellbeing. I realized that awareness was not just about inner thoughts; it was also about how those thoughts shaped my emotional responses and relationships.

Yung Pueblo's (2021) *Clarity & Connection* echoed these lessons in a spiritual frame: clarity emerges when we notice the patterns that repeat in our minds and hearts, and connection deepens when we act consciously from that awareness. My childhood, filled with scarcity and improvisation, was my first laboratory for these insights. I was learning to navigate limitation with creativity, to process emotions with intention, and to connect with others even when circumstances were difficult.

The Sacred NeuroReset Method: Creating Flow and Mental Freedom

Looking back, I can see that I was practicing many of the principles Mihaly Csikszentmihalyi (1990) describes in *Flow* long before I knew his research existed. I lost myself in the act of imagining, creating, and exploring, even when the world around me felt small or constrained. Mud pies, rain puddles, sketched stories, and imagined cities were all exercises in focused attention, intrinsic motivation, and deep engagement. I learned that mental freedom doesn't require perfect conditions; it requires presence, curiosity, and a willingness to immerse yourself fully in the process of creation.

These early exercises laid the foundation for my lifelong practice: observing my thoughts, noticing patterns, and choosing which story I wanted to live. Each day, each imagined adventure, each conscious breath became a step toward mental sovereignty—the ability to guide your mind rather than be led by it.

By combining imagination, observation, and conscious intention, I was learning the first principle of the Sacred NeuroReset Method: awareness is

"Mental freedom begins when you give yourself permission to reset your thoughts, not to have every answer, to simply be aware of your programming so that you can change it whenever you're ready."

the gateway to transformation. Before you can practice permission, healing, trust, alignment, and transformation, you must first awaken to the fact that your mind is not the master of your life; it is a tool for your liberation.

The childhood moments I shared—mud pies, puddle reflections, imagined cities—were exercises in neural rewiring, long before I understood the science.

Awakening Ritual

Awakening is the first step in the Sacred NeuroReset Method; a practice of recognizing that your mind is a storyteller, not your master. Through this ritual, you cultivate the awareness that your thoughts are not your truth; they are signals, reflections, and opportunities to create consciously.

Step 1: Observe Your Thoughts (5–10 Minutes)

- Find a quiet space where you can sit comfortably. Close your eyes and take several deep, grounding breaths.
- Simply notice your thoughts as they arise, like clouds drifting across the sky. Avoid judging them, labeling them, or trying to change them; just witness them.
- Pay attention to patterns, recurring themes, or emotional triggers. Notice which thoughts spark tension, anxiety, or limitation.

Step 2: Journal Your Stories

- Open your journal and write down the recurring stories your mind tells you, especially those that hold you back or create fear.
- Include the emotions attached to each story. For example, "I'm not good enough" may bring sadness, anxiety, or shame.
- Reflect on where these stories may have originated—childhood, societal expectations, or past experiences—and honor that they were once necessary survival tools.

Step 3: Choose One Story to Rewrite

- Select one limiting story to transform. Ask yourself, "What version of this story would reflect hope, growth, and possibility?"
- Write a new narrative as if it has already been realized. For example, "I am not good enough" becomes "I am fully capable, worthy, and equipped to create the life I desire."
- Add sensory details: how it feels, looks, and sounds when this new story is true. The more vivid, the stronger the neural imprint.

Step 4: Speak, Feel, and Visualize

- Read your rewritten story aloud with intention and conviction. Let the words resonate in your body, chest, and heart.
- Close your eyes and imagine the story unfolding in your life. See yourself acting, receiving, and thriving in alignment with this new narrative.
- Anchor it with a physical gesture (a hand over your heart, lifting your arms, or placing your hands on your knees) to signal your nervous system that this is your truth.

Step 5: Integrate Through Breath

- After speaking and visualizing, take three slow, deep breaths, letting the new story settle into your mind and body.
- Inhale possibility. Exhale old limitations. Repeat until you feel a sense of peace, alignment, or inspiration.

Optional Amplifiers

- Light a candle or incense during the ritual to symbolize illumination and clarity.
- Play soft, calming music or a frequency that resonates with your intention.
- Return to this ritual weekly to strengthen the new neural pathway, reinforcing your ability to author your thoughts and life consciously.

> *"Every time you pause before reacting, question a limiting belief, or choose stillness over spiraling, you're practicing mental wellbeing."*

Reflection Prompts Imagine your mind as a vast canvas. Which colors, textures, and patterns are you painting right now? If you could cocreate with your higher self, what masterpiece would emerge?

Permission—Grant Yourself Mental Freedom

Permission is a radical act of self-liberation. In a world that often rewards conformity, productivity, and perfection, allowing yourself to pause, explore, and question can feel revolutionary. Giving yourself permission is not indulgence; it's reclaiming your mind, your story, and your soul's authority.

> *"Mental freedom begins the moment you realize you can rewrite your story at any time, no matter what has happened in your past."*

It's the sacred acknowledgment that you can rewrite your story at any stage of life. It's the grace of allowing your mind to wander, your heart to feel, and your soul to lead.

Reframing Limiting Beliefs Ritual

This ritual is your tool for embodying permission. It guides you to recognize old stories, release what no longer serves you, and rewire your mind for possibility.

Step 1: Identify Your Limiting Beliefs

- Quiet your mind and ask, "Which thoughts consistently hold me back or create fear?"
- Write them down without judgment. Common examples include the following:
  - "I should have figured this out by now."
  - "I don't have time to prioritize myself."
  - "I'm not enough."

- Notice the emotions attached to these beliefs: guilt, shame, anxiety, or doubt.

Step 2: Seek the Hidden Liberation

- For each limiting belief, ask, "What liberating truth or affirmation is waiting beneath this story?"
- Turn restriction into possibility. For example:
  - **Limiting belief:** "I've missed my chance to create the life I want."
  - **Liberating affirmation:** "I am always capable of growth, reinvention, and creating new possibilities, no matter my age or circumstances."
- Trust that your mind can accept new pathways; this is neuroplasticity in action.

Step 3: Speak, Feel, and Embody

- Speak your liberating affirmation aloud, slowly, and intentionally. Feel the vibration in your body.
- Place your hands over your heart, chest, or belly, wherever it feels grounding, as you repeat the affirmation.
- Visualize the belief transforming: Imagine the old story dissolving and your new truth radiating through your thoughts, posture, and energy.

Step 4: Journal the Shift

- Write a paragraph or a few sentences about how your day, choices, or perspective would change if this liberating belief were your default.
- Note any emotional shifts or insights that arise; this strengthens the neural and energetic imprint of the new story.

Step 5: Integrate Through Breath

- Follow your affirmation practice with the Seven Sacred Breaths: Inhale possibility, hold, exhale limitations. Repeat seven times.
- Let each breath anchor your mind in freedom, opening your awareness to creative solutions and joy.

"Healing your mind begins when you stop believing every thought you think and start listening for the silent wisdom underneath it."

Healing—Listening to the Silent Wisdom

Healing begins not by chasing every thought, but by tuning into the subtle wisdom that whispers beneath the surface. Before I could cook, I practiced creation with mud pies. Those early moments taught me that the act of imagining, creating, and surrendering to the flow of possibility was a form of healing the current state of my mind that was only based on circumstances.

Today, I invite you to bring that same sacred attention to your thoughts. Imagine creating a nourishing meal in your mind, or envisioning a project, experience, or relationship coming to life. See it, smell it, feel it fully. This is more than visualization; it's a sacred act of cocreation, training your brain to imagine without fear, to create without limitation, and to trust the guidance of your inner wisdom.

The Seven Sacred Breaths Ritual

Breath is the invisible thread connecting body, mind, and soul. It carries you from overwhelm to clarity and from tension to peace. Through intentional, sacred breathing, you can reshape neural pathways, release limiting thoughts, and anchor yourself in presence.

Step 1: Inhale Possibility Breathe in through your nose for four counts, imagining life, creativity, and abundance flowing into your being.

Step 2: Hold and Anchor Hold your breath for four counts, feeling the energy settle into your body. This pause enables your nervous system to integrate the inhale, planting seeds of peace and focus.

Step 3: Exhale Limitations Slowly exhale through your mouth for six counts, releasing tension, fear, and limiting thoughts. Imagine every exhale washing away what no longer serves you.

Step 4: Repeat the Cycle Seven Times Each round strengthens your mind-body connection and deepens your capacity for presence. The number seven is sacred; symbolizing completion, wholeness, and alignment.

Daily Healing Integration To make the Seven Sacred Breaths a true reset:

- Visualize a desired experience, project, or emotion in vivid detail.
- Notice thoughts, feelings, and bodily sensations as they arise; observe without judgment.
- Journal insights: what does this reveal about your creative capacity, resilience, or inner guidance?
- Follow with the Seven Sacred Breaths to integrate clarity, peace, and focus.

The Joy Ritual

1. **Make a joy list:** Write down every activity, big or small, that brings you joy: listening to music, playing basketball, cooking, walking in nature, painting, dancing in your living room.
2. **Choose three each day:** Commit to doing at least three joyful things daily, no matter how small.
3. **Savor them fully:** Don't just check them off; immerse yourself. Feel the music, taste the food, breathe the fresh air. Let joy flood your body.
4. **Visualize alignment:** As you do these joyful things, imagine your energy radiating outward, calling in opportunities aligned with your soul.

Jamal's Story

When Jamal first came to me, he carried a heavy fog of disappointment and exhaustion. Corporate layoffs had left him without the stability he thought was secure. He pursued every opportunity with determination, but as rejection piled up, his confidence crumbled.

He wasn't just unemployed; he was unraveling. Some days he didn't want to get out of bed. His workouts stopped. Healthy habits

(*continued*)

(continued)

disappeared. He turned to late-night snacking, endless streaming, and numbing routines. His attempts at entrepreneurship felt hollow. "What's the point?" he asked, eyes full of defeat.

I recognized that feeling; I had been there myself. I shared with Jamal a time when I felt completely lost. No matter how hard I worked, nothing clicked. The shift didn't come from chasing harder. It came when I stopped, turned inward, and did one simple thing: I followed my joy.

I encouraged him to fill his days with rituals that lifted his energy—singing, yoga, creating, laughing, and spending time in nature. Alongside these joys, he practiced the Seven Sacred Breaths whenever tension, fear, or frustration arose. The Joy Ritual is simple yet powerful.

Jamal resisted at first. "How is shooting hoops or cooking dinner going to get me a job?" he asked. But he trusted me enough to try. And that was when the shift began.

He started with simple things: jogging in the morning sun, cooking the healthy meals he loved, and playing guitar in the evenings. Slowly, he added more, catching up with friends, volunteering, taking long hikes. Alongside these joys, he practiced the Seven Sacred Breaths to calm his mind and reset when fear tried to creep back in. Day by day, his vibration lifted.

It didn't happen overnight, but within weeks, Jamal noticed something had changed. His laughter came back. His posture shifted. His conversations carried lightness instead of despair. He began visualizing himself thriving—not from desperation, but from genuine excitement.

Then one afternoon, out of the blue, a former colleague reached out about a position. It wasn't just any job, it was his dream job, aligned with his skills, passions, and purpose. Jamal showed up to the interview with confidence, clarity, and grounded energy, and he landed it.

Jamal's story is a reminder: opportunities align when your energy aligns. When you lift yourself out of fear and despair through joy, you become magnetic to the life you're meant to live.

The mind responds to ritual, alignment, and breath. When you clear the noise, release tension, and embody presence, your inner wisdom guides you toward life's flow.

"Peace of mind is borne not from controlling your thoughts, but from trusting that your awareness is greater than anything your mind creates."

Reflection Prompts

- What patterns arise when I visualize abundance or success?
- Which fears surface, and how can I gently redirect them?
- How does my body respond to creative rehearsal versus stress-induced rumination?

"Healing your mind begins when you learn to listen beneath the noise, to the wisdom quietly waiting."

Trust—Peace of Mind Through Awareness

Trust transforms the mind from adversary to ally. When we observe thoughts without reacting, we create space for intuition, clarity, and alignment with our higher self to emerge. Trust is the bridge between mental freedom and soul-led guidance; it allows the mind to be a tool rather than a tyrant.

Pause Trust Ritual

This ritual is designed to cultivate inner peace, anchor presence, and strengthen your capacity to respond rather than react.

Step 1: Pause and Center

- When triggered, overwhelmed, or anxious, pause completely. Step away from distractions or stop whatever you're doing.
- Close your eyes, soften your shoulders, and feel your connection to the present moment.

Step 2: Conscious Breath

- Take three slow, deep breaths. Inhale through the nose for four counts, hold for four counts, exhale through the mouth for six counts.
- With each exhale, release tension, judgment, and mental noise. With each inhale, invite clarity, peace, and self-trust.

Step 3: Ask Your Mind

- Silently or aloud, ask, "What is my mind guiding me toward?"
- Observe the first impressions, images, or sensations without trying to fix or analyze them.

Step 4: Release and Affirm

- Allow thoughts to float past like clouds. Don't attach to the story; simply notice it.
- Whisper an intentional affirmation: "I choose peace. I choose me. I trust my awareness above all else."

Step 5: Integrate Through Breath

- If frustration or anxiety persists, follow the pause with the Seven Sacred Breaths: Inhale possibility, hold, exhale limitations, repeating seven times.
- Feel the energy of each exhale washing away mental clutter, while each inhale anchors your presence, intention, and inner alignment.

Leah's Story: Radical Self-Love Through Trust

When Leah first came to me, she felt lost. After a devastating betrayal, her world collapsed. She stopped eating regularly, abandoned her workout routine, and picked up smoking again after years of being free from it. She whispered during our first session, "I don't even know who I am anymore."

Her mind was trapped in a relentless loop:

- "How could he do this?"
- "Why wasn't I enough?"
- "Maybe I'll never trust again."

While her ex had caused undeniable harm, Leah's choices were now compounding her pain.

One day I gently said, "This person hurt you deeply. But right now, you're hurting yourself even more." Tears came. She realized she had abandoned herself in the wake of being abandoned.

I invited her to imagine radical self-love: What if you started treating yourself as if you were the love of your life?

At first, it felt foreign to her. Leah had invested so much of her worth in someone else's love that turning inward seemed impossible. Slowly, we began with a ritual of apology and forgiveness through transformational letter writing:

- To herself: She apologized for neglecting her health and silencing her needs.
- To her ex: She didn't excuse his actions, but released resentment.
- To her health: Forgiveness has been associated with reduced stress responses and improved cardiovascular markers (van Oyen Witvliet et al., 2001).
- To her future self: She affirmed her commitment to joy, health, and unconditional self-love.

With each word, Leah released anger and reclaimed her power.

Next, she incorporated the Pause Trust Ritual whenever thoughts spiraled:

- Pause.
- Take three deep, conscious breaths.
- Whisper "I choose peace. I choose me."

(*continued*)

(*continued*)

She replaced cigarettes with the Seven Sacred Breaths. She inhaled peace and exhaled grief. Movement returned, not as punishment, but as devotion to her body. She nourished herself with intentional meals, making eating a ritual of care rather than neglect.

Months later, Leah radiated joy, saying: "I don't just want love, I am love." Her transformation wasn't about erasing betrayal; it was about transmuting it into wisdom, strength, and deep self-respect.

"Forgiveness doesn't excuse the past; it frees your future."

"When your thoughts align with truth and love, your mind becomes a servant of your soul and clarity becomes your natural state."

Integration Insights

- Trust strengthens the prefrontal cortex, enhancing emotional regulation, decision-making, and problem-solving.
- Each pause, breath, and affirmation becomes a micro-ritual, rewiring neural pathways for clarity, intentional action, and self-compassion.

Practice—Applying Mental Wellbeing Daily

Every time you pause before reacting, question a limiting belief, or choose stillness over spiraling, you're practicing mental wellbeing.

Consistency transforms thought into power. Daily sacred rituals ensure that your mind becomes a tool of creativity, insight, and resilience rather than a source of stress. Mental wellbeing is not a one-time achievement, it's a sacred practice, a daily ritual of conscious attention.

Maya's Story: A Post-Divorce Transformation

Maya came to me after her divorce, feeling exhausted, frustrated, and unsure of how to navigate co-parenting, her career, and her own emotional wellbeing. Every message from her ex-spouse triggered anxiety, every decision felt heavier than it should, and she struggled to find clarity amid the chaos. She knew she wanted transformation but she didn't know where to start.

We began by focusing on pausing before reacting, a foundational principle in mental wellbeing. I introduced Maya to the Pause Trust Ritual, a sacred ritual to stop emotional reactivity and observe her thoughts without judgment:

- Pause when stressed or triggered.
- Take three deep, conscious breaths.
- Ask, "What is my mind guiding me toward?"
- Observe without judgment and release.
- If frustration persisted, use the Seven Sacred Breaths to restore clarity.

At first, it was challenging. Her instincts were to respond immediately, to defend, to control. But with consistency, Maya noticed a shift: She began to respond consciously rather than reacting from fear or anger. Her co-parenting interactions became calmer, more effective, and more compassionate.

Next, we worked on granting herself permission to reset her thoughts. Divorce often brings guilt, self-doubt, and the feeling that you've "failed." I guided Maya through the Permission Ritual:

- Identify a recurring limiting belief, such as "I'm failing as a parent."
- Ask, "What liberating affirmation lies hidden here?"
- She spoke it aloud, wrote it in her journal, and let it resonate in her body.

(continued)

(continued)

Maya's liberating affirmation became "I am capable of growth, reinvention, and creating new possibilities, no matter what happened in the past." Saying this daily gave her the courage to explore new hobbies, relationships, and career paths, reminding her that her story was still hers to write.

Through mindful observation and cognitive reframing, Maya began noticing her thought patterns, especially the fear-driven ones. She would pause, ask, "Is this true? Is this serving me?" and consciously shift her thinking. Each small act (pausing, journaling, breathing) retrained her mind to become an ally instead of an adversary.

Over time, Maya's mental landscape transformed. Where there was once chaos and self-doubt, there was now clarity, empowerment, and alignment with her highest self. She developed the confidence to set boundaries, prioritized her emotional wellbeing, and co-parented with patience and love.

"Every sacred ritual practiced daily is a seed planted in your mind, growing into peace, clarity, and empowerment."

Alignment—Harmonizing Thoughts and Soul

When your thoughts align with truth and love, your mind becomes a servant of your soul, and clarity becomes your natural state.

Alignment begins as awareness and culminates in transformation. Through conscious thought, elevated emotion, and sacred practice, you move from chaos to coherence, where your mind, body, and spirit harmonize to create the reality your soul envisions.

Alignment is cultivated through journaling, affirmations, and intentional thought selection. By bringing awareness to your mental patterns, you learn to recognize chaos, release limitations, and choose thoughts that nurture growth, creativity, and inner peace.

Daily Alignment Ritual

1. **Morning:** Identify your top three intentions for the day.
2. **Observe:** Notice any mental chatter or distractions that pull you off course.
3. **Redirect:** Pause, breathe, and realign with your purpose.
4. **Evening:** Journal reflections on how your thoughts, actions, and energy aligned with your intentions.

Mid-life often brings the challenge of juggling multiple priorities; career, family, relationships, and self-care. Alignment rituals serve as your compass, helping you discern which thoughts and actions truly serve your highest purpose in each season of life.

> *"The journey from chaos to clarity is paved with small, sacred rituals practiced with intention and love."*

The most sacred journey of the mind is moving from chaos to clarity, from fear-driven thoughts to soul-led wisdom.

Childhood scarcity taught me resilience. Mud pies and daydreams taught me creation. Each thought I nurtured, each belief I shifted, built the bridge from mental survival to soulful transformation.

Sacred Transformation

Modern neuroscience confirms what ancient wisdom has long known: Transformation begins in the mind.

Dr. Joe Dispenza (2013) and other researchers reveal that pairing ritual with elevated emotion, visualization, and focused attention rewires neural pathways, turning alignment into embodied transformation.

Brain Rewiring Rituals

1. **Elevated Emotion Ritual:** Pair visualization with gratitude, joy, or love to anchor new neural patterns.
2. **Mental Rehearsal Ritual:** Rehearse experiences you wish to manifest, training your brain to expect alignment.
3. **Heart-Brain Coherence Ritual:** Breathwork and visualization bring your nervous system into harmony.
4. **Interruption Ritual:** Break unhelpful thought loops through conscious breathing, journaling, or meditation.
5. **Brain Reset Ritual:** Use your nondominant hand for small tasks to awaken new neural pathways.

Daily Integration Example

- **Morning:** Ten-minute visualization of your ideal day infused with elevated emotion
- **Midday:** Five-minute observation of thoughts plus Seven Sacred Breaths ritual reset
- **Evening:** Reflective journaling on how your day aligned with your soul's highest vision

> *"Rituals practiced with awareness are the bridge between the mind's chaos, the soul's clarity, and the body's transformation."*

Alignment becomes transformation when thought becomes action and belief becomes being.

Through consistent rituals, you rewire your mind, regulate your emotions, and restore your natural rhythm of joy and peace. Transformation is not a destination; it is the daily unfolding of your true self.

Reflection Prompts

- Which thoughts am I unconsciously repeating that hold me back?
- How does my mind influence my emotional and physical wellbeing?
- When I pause and breathe, what new insights or solutions emerge?
- How can I nurture my creative potential daily?
- Which rituals resonate most deeply, and how can I make them consistent?
- How do my beliefs about age, purpose, or success shape my growth?

Closing Blessing

May you be gentle with your thoughts and patient with your mind.

May you see each thought as a sacred messenger, not a dictator of destiny.

May your mind become a sanctuary of clarity, creativity, and peace.

Remember:

- You are aware.
- You are capable.
- You are transforming.
- You are free.

> *"The most sacred journey of the mind is moving from chaos to clarity, from fear-driven thoughts to soul-led wisdom."*

Optional Exploration: Deepening Your Mental Wellbeing

Breaking the Habit of Being Yourself, Joe Dispenza. Combines neuroscience and meditation to reprogram limiting beliefs and create new patterns of thought.

Living in Wisdom, Devi Brown. Invites readers to deepen their inner awareness and integrate mindfulness into daily decision-making.

Good Vibes, Good Life, Vex King. Offers mindset tools to replace negativity with self-love and attract higher vibrational experiences.

The Power of Now, Eckhart Tolle. A modern spiritual classic on presence, teaching how to quiet the mind and live in the moment.

Nothing Is Missing, Nicole Walters. A story of reinvention and self-discovery that redefines success and reminds us that we already have enough.

Feeding the Soul, Tabitha Brown. Blends stories, wisdom, and affirmations to nurture mental peace and joy through faith and authenticity.

Radical Confidence, Lisa Bilyeu. Empowers readers to move through fear and self-doubt by taking bold, consistent action toward growth.

These resources illuminate practices, perspectives, and rituals to help you train your mind, cultivate clarity, and sustain mental wellbeing. True wisdom lives within your awareness, your daily rituals, and your commitment to alignment.

References

Brown, B. (2021). *Atlas of the heart: Mapping meaningful connection and the language of human experience*. Random House.

Csikszentmihalyi, M. (1990). *Flow: The psychology of optimal experience*. Harper & Row.

David, S. (2016). *Emotional agility: Get unstuck, embrace change, and thrive in work and life*. Avery.

Doidge, N. (2007). *The brain that changes itself: Stories of personal triumph from the frontiers of brain science*. Viking.

Dispenza, J. (2013). *Breaking the habit of being yourself: How to lose your mind and create a new one*. Hay House.

Dweck, C. S. (2006). *Mindset: The new psychology of success*. Random House.

King, V. (2018). *Good vibes, good life: How self-love is the key to unlocking your greatness*. Hay House UK.

Pueblo, Y. (2021). *Clarity & connection*. Andrews McMeel Publishing.

Tolle, E. (1997). *The power of now: A guide to spiritual enlightenment*. New World Library.

van Oyen Witvliet, C., Ludwig, T. E., & Vander Laan, K. L. (2001). Granting forgiveness or harboring grudges: Implications for emotion, physiology, and health. *Psychological Science, 12*(2), 117–123.

4 Nutritional Wellbeing

Tohamina / Freepik

Nourishment as Self-Love

Food is not just fuel; it's the most intimate form of self-love.

For most of my life, food was something I consumed almost unconsciously. My choices were dictated by taste, culture, and convenience. I grew up believing that a proper meal always included meat, a starch, and a handful of vegetables. Meals were measured not by nourishment but by familiarity. I didn't think much beyond filling my stomach or satisfying my cravings, and I rarely considered how food could shape my body, my mind, or even the energy I carried through my day.

But as my journey into healing deepened, everything changed. Eating disorders challenged my body and mind. A period of veganism expanded my consciousness, teaching me to notice not just what I ate but how I felt, thought, and interacted with the world around me. Later, my fertility journey forced me to confront questions I had never considered: What is food really? Is it merely fuel, or could it carry energy, information, and medicine?

Could the simple act of placing a meal on my plate influence my womb, my hormonal balance, my mental clarity, and even my spiritual connection?

Through trial, error, and moments of deep awakening, I discovered a profound truth: Plants are more than nourishment; they are sacred messengers. Each leaf, root, seed, and fruit carries light codes from the sun, minerals from the earth, and water from the sky. Each bite is an invitation to align with nature's intelligence and wisdom, to remember that every meal is a dialogue with life itself. Choosing a plant-based way of eating became one of the most empowering, transformative, and grounding rituals of my life.

But before I fully understood the science and spirituality of plants, my relationship with food expressed itself in a different way—through creativity, community, and celebration.

Tip: The practices shared in this chapter are offered for inspiration and education only. Everybody is different. Please listen to your body and consult with your doctor or a qualified healthcare professional before making changes to your diet, fasting, or wellness routine, especially if you have existing health conditions or specific dietary needs.

Food as Community and Celebration

My first self-published book, *Koya's Kuisine: Foods You Love That Love You Back,* was born from a simple but powerful desire: to show people that healthy eating could be both nourishing and joyful. In that book, I shared recipes that didn't just taste good but also loved you back, supporting the mind, body, and soul. It wasn't about restriction or deprivation; it was about remembering that food can be medicine, pleasure, and connection all at once.

About the same time, I started hosting monthly dinner parties that became an extension of this philosophy. These weren't just meals; they were immersive experiences. Imagine a five- to seven-course plant-based feast for 40 guests, each dish crafted to awaken the senses and fuel the body with healing ingredients. The table became more than a place to eat; it was a sacred gathering space where people connected through food, conversation, and presence.

But it wasn't only about the food. Each evening also included live music, fashion shows, and a sense of artistry woven into every detail. The meals were the heart of it, but the energy was communal, creative, and celebratory. People left not only full but also inspired, uplifted, and more deeply connected to themselves and others.

> *"Food is not just fuel; it's the most intimate form of self-love."*

These dinner parties were my first taste of what it means to create a community grounded in food that heals. I witnessed firsthand how a meal could be transformational. Guests would tell me that they felt lighter, more energized, or even more emotionally open after eating consciously prepared plant-based meals. I began to see food not just as something we consume but as a bridge, a way to connect people to themselves, to each other, and to the greater wisdom of nature.

Looking back, I recognize how those gatherings planted the seeds for everything I now teach about nutritional wellbeing. They taught me that healing doesn't have to be quiet or solitary; it can be joyful, celebratory, and shared. Food, when prepared and served with love, becomes more than sustenance; it becomes a ritual of connection and remembrance. It reminds us that every bite is part of a larger story of community, creativity, and collective healing.

This lived experience became the foundation for my deeper exploration into the science and spirituality of food. What I once practiced intuitively, I would later discover to be affirmed by both modern research and ancient wisdom.

Science and Spirit

Modern science validates what our ancestors intuitively knew for centuries. A diet rich in whole-plant foods has been shown to do the following:

- Lower inflammation, reducing the risk of chronic diseases including diabetes, cardiovascular disease, and autoimmune conditions
- Balance hormones, supporting fertility, healthy menstrual cycles, and adrenal function
- Support heart, liver, and gut health, crucial organs in detoxification, metabolism, and overall vitality
- Promote longevity, enhancing quality of life by supporting cellular health, reducing oxidative stress, and maintaining optimal metabolic function

For women navigating fertility or healing journeys, plants are particularly potent. Phytonutrients, antioxidants, and fiber nurture the womb, regulate cycles, and detoxify the body of heavy metals and excess estrogen (Kan et al., 2022). Flavonoids in colorful fruits, the indoles in cruciferous vegetables, and polyphenols in leafy greens have measurable effects on estrogen metabolism and inflammatory signaling, supporting reproductive health in ways that modern medicine is only beginning to fully appreciate.

Yet beyond the measurable science lies the soul benefit. Plants are alive with vibration. When we consume fruits, vegetables, legumes, grains, seeds, and nuts in their most natural, unprocessed state, we absorb not just their nutrients but also their frequency. This subtle energy can attune us to higher states of consciousness, creativity, empathy, and compassion.

Food is frequency. Plants carry a high vibration. When eaten mindfully, the act of consuming them is an intimate form of energetic alignment. Every bite is an opportunity to cultivate harmony with body, mind, and spirit. This is why nutrition, when approached with intention, can feel as much like meditation as it does like sustenance.

Healing Through Connection

Every culture on Earth has revered the sacred relationship between humans and plants.

- Indigenous traditions view plants as teachers, allies, and guides for healing. Shamans and medicine women would consult plants for guidance, using them as tools to restore balance in body, mind, and spirit. Plants were never just food; they were living entities with wisdom to share.
- In traditional Chinese medicine, foods are understood in terms of energetic qualities: warming or cooling, yin or yang. Each ingredient harmonizes organ systems, supports the flow of qi, and maintains balance in the body's subtle energies.
- In Ayurveda, foods are categorized according to how they influence the doshas—*vata*, *pitta*, and *kapha*. The qualities of food, their taste, texture, and energy, directly affect body and mind, supporting digestion, mental clarity, and emotional equilibrium.

When we choose a plant-based way of eating, we reconnect with this ancient lineage of wisdom. We remember that food is grown, not manufactured. That a seed carries the memory of the tree it will become, that the fruit carries the sweetness of the sun, and that each meal is a conduit of life force energy.

> *"Every bite you take is a message you send to your future body."*

Every time you pause to bless your meal, you honor the chain of life—from the soil beneath your feet to the temple of your body. Eating is not merely functional; it is a sacred act of alignment, gratitude, and love. By acknowledging the source of our food, we begin to cultivate reverence for the Earth, the ecosystems that sustain us, and the complex network of energy and nutrients that feed every cell in our body.

The Body as a Sacred Temple

When we eat mindfully, our food choices ripple through every system of our body. Consider the gut, often called the *second brain.* The micro-biome (trillions of microorganisms in our digestive tract) is directly influenced by diet. Whole-plant foods provide prebiotic fiber, which feeds beneficial bacteria and supports immune function, mental clarity, and mood regulation. Research increasingly shows that a healthy micro-biome is foundational for hormonal balance, fertility, and emotional resilience.

Nutrients like magnesium, zinc, and vitamin C, abundant in colorful plant foods, are vital for enzyme function, hormone synthesis, and cellular repair. Omega-3 fatty acids from algae, chia, and flax reduce inflammation, support brain function, and modulate stress response. Even the vibration of plants, the subtle energy we absorb during mindful consumption, may influence neurotransmitter activity and emotional regulation.

This is why nutrition cannot be separated from spiritual practice. Eating plants mindfully is an act of self-respect and reverence, a daily meditation that reminds us our bodies are sacred, resilient, and intelligent.

One client came to me with hormonal imbalance and anxiety. She was chronically fatigued, her cycles irregular, and her connection to her body was minimal. After many doctor visits and still no answers, we explored slowing down at mealtimes, choosing whole-plant foods, and seed cycling (eating specific seeds at different points in the menstrual cycle to support hormone balance). Within weeks, she reported feeling lighter, more grounded, and energetically aligned. Her intuition sharpened, and she began making decisions in life with clarity and intention—a living example of how nutrition ripples outward into mind, body, and spirit.

> *"Listen to your body; it whispers what your mind tries to ignore."*

Plants as Sacred Messengers

Plants are not inert matter; they are living intelligence. They sense, respond, and communicate. Their colors, aromas, and textures are designed to draw humans into a state of receptivity, joy, and connection. When we eat a carrot or sip a green smoothie, we are literally receiving energy that has been stored and amplified through photosynthesis—light transformed into nourishment.

- Green leaves, rich in chlorophyll, signal detoxification and cellular regeneration.
- Red fruits, high in anthocyanins and lycopene, support heart and reproductive health.
- Yellow and orange produce, abundant in carotenoids, enhance immune function and mood regulation.

Every meal is a conversation between our cells and the life force embedded in our food. By choosing plants consciously, we are aligning ourselves with the intelligence of life itself.

Another client, a woman navigating fertility challenges, began incorporating high-vibration plant foods, ritualized meal blessings, and conscious hydration. Within two months, not only did her energy increase but also her cycles became more regular and she reported deeper emotional resilience. She described feeling as though her body was "remembering how to thrive," and her connection to the natural rhythms of life deepened in ways that no medical test could quantify.

Witnessing transformational stories based in nutrition remind us that nutrition is not just about sustenance; it is a tool for transformation, healing, and empowerment. It is a daily practice that touches every facet of our being: physical, emotional, and spiritual.

Food as Frequency

Scientific studies increasingly explore the bioenergetics of food, showing that the vibrational quality of plant-based foods influences cellular signaling, hormonal balance, and emotional states. While traditional nutrition focuses on macronutrients and micronutrients, modern research suggests that the energetic quality of food; its frequency, may also influence wellbeing. Eating high-vibration foods can increase mental clarity, emotional resilience, and spiritual attunement, creating a feedback loop of health and consciousness.

The Ritual of Gratitude

Every time you bless your meal, you honor the chain of life—from the soil beneath your feet to your sacred body temple. This ritual is simple yet profound—pause, breathe, and acknowledge the energy, effort, and intelligence that created your meal. Gratitude amplifies the nourishment, deepening your body's ability to receive, digest, and transform food into fuel.

Seven Sacred Nutritional Wellbeing Rituals

These seven sacred nutritional rituals are simple intentional ways of nurturing the body while honoring food as medicine. Each ritual invites you to slow down, listen inwardly, and transform eating into an act of self-care.

The Eat More Plants Ritual

A plant-based ritual doesn't have to be about perfection, restriction, or strict rules. It is a practice of intention, reverence, and alignment. By choosing plants mindfully, you are not only nourishing your body but also honoring the intelligence of life, the energy of the earth, and your own creative and healing potential.This ritual is a simple, sacred way to bring mindfulness and vibrancy into your daily nutrition.

Why It Matters **Health:** Plants provide an unparalleled array of essential nutrients, antioxidants, and fiber that support longevity, vitality, and disease prevention. Diets rich in vegetables, fruits, legumes, whole grains, seeds, and nuts help regulate blood sugar, reduce inflammation, and support hormonal balance. This kind of mindful eating strengthens not just the body but also the mind and spirit, giving us clarity, resilience, and a deeper connection to our inner wisdom.

Compassion: Choosing plant-based foods aligns our actions with kindness and empathy toward all living beings. Each plant-based meal is a conscious choice to reduce harm, honor life, and embrace the principle of nonviolence. This practice cultivates a heart-centered approach to consumption, where the energy we bring to our meals reverberates in our daily interactions and relationships.

Planetary care: Eating plants contributes to the preservation and healing of our planet. Plant-based diets significantly reduce greenhouse gas emissions, conserve freshwater, and decrease deforestation caused by livestock production. By making conscious food choices, we become active participants in the restoration and protection of Earth's ecosystems, contributing to a future in which both humans and nature thrive.

Global impact: Redirecting resources from livestock production toward growing crops for direct human consumption has the potential to address hunger and food insecurity worldwide. Every mindful meal becomes a ripple in a larger movement toward equitable and sustainable food systems, reminding us that our choices matter on a global scale.

Sustainability: Supporting regenerative agriculture practices restores soil health, promotes biodiversity, and strengthens local ecosystems. When we choose foods cultivated with care for the land and the communities that nurture them, we are investing in long-term planetary health. Conscious consumption is therefore not only an act of personal wellbeing but also a tangible expression of stewardship for the generations that follow.

By approaching meals with reverence, gratitude, and intention, we transform eating into a ritual of connection, healing, and contribution. Each bite becomes a prayer, a statement of values, and a deliberate alignment with life itself. Conscious consumption is a daily practice that nourishes not just the body but also the heart, mind, and soul, weaving together health, compassion, and planetary responsibility in every meal.

How to Eat More Plants

1. **Morning reset:** Begin your day with fruit, water, and light liquids only until noon. This is a practice that honors your body's natural detox cycles and gives your digestive system a gentle reset. Starting your morning in this way floods your system with hydration, enzymes, and life force energy, while allowing your body to awaken gently. Imagine each sip and each bite as sunlight transforming into vitality within you. Citrus, berries, melon, or a green juice can be particularly energizing. Notice the clarity and lightness that comes from beginning your day in harmony with your body's natural rhythms.
2. **Rainbow plate:** With every main meal, aim for at least three colors of plants. Let your plate look like a vibrant slice of nature's palette:
   - Greens for healing, growth, and balance
   - Reds for vitality, circulation, and life force

- Yellows and oranges for joy, warmth, and creative energy
- Purples for intuition, clarity, and spiritual attunement

   By intentionally choosing color and variety, you are inviting diversity into your cells, flooding your body with a spectrum of phytonutrients, antioxidants, and vibrational energy. Eating this way transforms meals into a multisensory experience, a ritual in which your plate becomes a canvas and every bite a brushstroke of wellness.

3. **Sacred gratitude pause:** Before you eat, pause and place your hands over your food. Take one deep, intentional breath and offer a blessing: "Thank you, God, for this nourishment. May it heal my body, mind, and soul."

   This moment of acknowledgment elevates the act of eating into a sacred exchange, reminding you that every plant, every bite, is a gift from the Earth and the Universe. Gratitude is a high-frequency practice; it opens your body to absorption, your mind to clarity, and your heart to joy.
4. **Core alignment:** As you chew, bring awareness to your womb space or solar plexus. Visualize the nutrients being absorbed there first, nourishing your center of creativity, intuition, and vitality. This is a practice of internal alignment, connecting the physical act of eating to your energetic body. Each bite becomes a conscious act of sending energy to your creative and life-giving centers, reinforcing the sacred relationship between nutrition and personal empowerment.
5. **Closing reflection:** After finishing your meal, pause again for one mindful breath. Observe how your body feels: energized, grounded, calm, or uplifted. Allow yourself to notice the subtle ways your body and energy shift as a result of intentional eating. Reflection completes the ritual, transforming a routine meal into a moment of spiritual nourishment.

Invitation to Practice Plant-Based Nutrition For the next seven days, commit to one plant-based meal per day. This could be a smoothie bowl, a vibrant salad, or a warm lentil soup. Notice the difference in your energy, mood, and clarity. Keep a journal and reflect daily on your experience.

Align and Deepen Practices

- **Mindful shopping:** Visit a local farmers market and choose produce intuitively. Let color, energy, and texture guide your selections.
- **Meal blessing:** Offer gratitude before each meal to elevate eating into a sacred ritual.
- **Cooking as meditation:** Prepare one meal in silence, letting chopping, stirring, and tasting become mindful practices.
- **Fasting with fruit:** Once a week, enjoy a fruit-only day to reset digestion and clear energy.

May every plant you consume be a prayer made visible. May your meals become meditations, your plate become an altar, and your body a temple renewed by the Earth's abundance. What you eat is not only fueling your cells, it is feeding your soul.

The Conscious Consumption Lifestyle

Every meal is more than nourishment; it is a sacred opportunity to honor the cycle of life. The act of eating is an intimate conversation with the planet, a moment to recognize the interconnected web of life that sustains us. The foods we choose carry energy, stories, and ripple effects that extend far beyond our plates. Every fruit, vegetable, grain, and seed is the culmination of sun, water, soil, and care, infused with life force energy. When we consciously select our meals, we are participating in a ritual of reciprocity, giving thanks for the abundance provided and acknowledging the intricate systems that make our sustenance possible.

Adopting a plant-based lifestyle is not just a dietary choice; it is an alignment of daily actions with health, compassion, and planetary stewardship. This ritual is a reminder that what we eat is a reflection of what we value and the energy we contribute to the world. Each meal becomes a deliberate prayer: a gesture of care for our bodies, the

(*continued*)

(*continued*)

animals, the Earth, and generations yet to come. It is a practice that transforms eating from a routine act into a spiritual and ethical engagement, blending nourishment with intention.

1. **Create a conscious meal:** Choose vibrant, whole-plant foods. Pause in gratitude for the sunlight, soil, water, and hands that brought them to you.
2. **Prepare with presence:** As you cook, notice the colors, textures, and aromas. Breathe deeply and set an intention: healing, joy, or connection with the Earth.
3. **Savor each bite:** Before eating, pause in appreciation. Chew slowly, taste fully, and tune into how your body responds.
4. **Reflect:** After the meal, notice your energy, mood, and clarity. Acknowledge the ways your choice supported not just your body but also life on Earth.

By honoring the cycle of life through conscious eating, we recognize that what nourishes us also sustains the world. Each bite becomes both self-care and sacred offering.

The Juice Feasting Ritual

Juice feasting is a transformative practice that floods your body with nutrients while giving the digestive system a much-needed rest. Unlike traditional fasting, where all food is restricted, juice *feasting* allows you to drink as much fresh, living juice as you need throughout the day. This practice nourishes the body at the cellular level, restores energy, and resets food patterns. But it is not just physical; it is a spiritual and emotional cleanse as well. By drinking fresh juice, you are receiving the essence of plants, minerals from the earth, water from the rain, and energy from the sun. Each glass becomes a liquid prayer, designed to awaken your body, clear your mind, and elevate your spirit.

"Nourishment gives you the power to show up as your highest self."

Why It Matters Juice feasting works on multiple layers:

- **Deep nourishment:** Juices provide vitamins, minerals, and antioxidants in their most bioavailable form, meaning your body absorbs nutrients quickly and efficiently.
- **Digestive rest:** With most fiber removed, your digestive system gets a break, freeing energy for cellular repair and rejuvenation.
- **Detoxification:** Fresh juices support the liver, kidneys, and lymphatic system in flushing out toxins and waste products.
- **Mental clarity:** Many people notice sharper focus, improved mood, and heightened intuition during juice feasts.
- **Emotional reset:** Juice feasting can help break cycles of emotional eating, allowing you to reconnect with food consciously.
- **Spiritual alignment:** Across cultures, fasting and feasting traditions remind us that simplifying what we consume creates space for spiritual insight and inner peace.

How to Practice Juice Feasting

1. **Set an intention:** Before you begin, ask yourself what you hope to receive: renewed energy, emotional release, or spiritual clarity. Your intention will guide the practice and elevate it beyond nutrition.
2. **Choose fresh, organic ingredients:** The quality of your produce determines the quality of your juice. Select organic, seasonal fruits and vegetables whenever possible.
3. **Juice in abundance:** Drink at least four to six 16-ounce servings daily. This is not about restriction; it is about abundance. Flood your body with light, living nutrition.
4. **Stay hydrated:** In addition to juices, drink plenty of pure water or herbal teas to support the cleansing process.
5. **Rest and reflect:** Allow your body to slow down. Journal your experiences, notice shifts in energy, and observe changes in mood and intuition.
6. **Break the feast gently:** When reintroducing solid foods, start with hydrating fruits, raw vegetables, or simple plant-based soups to honor your digestive system.

Seven Healing Juice Recipes Each recipe is carefully designed to support your body, mind, and spirit. Drink mindfully, imagining the energy of the plants flowing into every cell.

Green Glow Juice

Ingredients:

1 bunch kale (or spinach if kale is too strong)
1 cucumber
1 green apple
1 lemon, peeled
1-inch piece fresh ginger

Instructions: Wash all produce thoroughly. Juice, starting with leafy greens. Stir well and enjoy immediately.

Benefits: Packed with chlorophyll, iron, and vitamin C, this juice revitalizes blood, supports liver detox, and leaves you feeling vibrant and clear.

Beetroot Bliss

Ingredients:

2 medium beets
3 carrots
1 apple
1 lemon, peeled
1-inch piece fresh ginger

Instructions: Scrub beets and carrots. Juice all ingredients together. Stir and sip slowly.

Benefits: Beets improve circulation and stamina, supporting liver function. Combined with carrots and apple, this juice delivers cleansing, earthy sweetness.

Citrus Sunshine

Ingredients:

3 oranges, peeled
1 grapefruit, peeled
1 lemon, peeled
1-inch piece turmeric root (or ½ tsp turmeric powder)

Instructions: Juice citrus fruits with turmeric. Serve chilled.

Benefits: High in vitamin C for immune support and reduced inflammation; turmeric adds antioxidant and anti-inflammatory properties.

Tropical Carrot

Ingredients:

4 carrots
1 cup pineapple chunks
1-inch piece ginger
½ cup coconut water

Instructions: Juice carrots, pineapple, and ginger. Stir in coconut water. Serve over ice if desired.

Benefits: Carrots support eye and skin health, pineapple aids digestion, and ginger soothes and warms the digestive system.

Turmeric Tease

Ingredients:

2 oranges, peeled
1-inch piece turmeric root
1-inch piece ginger
1 pinch cayenne pepper

Instructions: Juice oranges, turmeric, and ginger. Add a pinch of cayenne. Stir and drink immediately.

Benefits: Reduces inflammation, boosts circulation, and awakens the senses. Cayenne enhances turmeric absorption and adds gentle heat to clear stagnation.

Berry Boost

Ingredients:

1 cup strawberries
1 cup blueberries
1 cup raspberries
1 apple
A few fresh mint leaves

Instructions: Wash berries. Juice berries, apple, and mint. Serve chilled.

Benefits: Antioxidant-rich, this juice protects cells from oxidative stress, supports brain and heart health, and energizes the spirit with sweetness and vibrancy.

Green Goodness

Ingredients:

1 bunch celery
2 cups spinach
1 cucumber
1 green apple
½ bunch parsley
1 lemon, peeled

Instructions: Wash all greens. Juice alternating soft and hard produce. Stir and drink fresh.

Benefits: This is a detox powerhouse supporting hydration, kidney health, and alkalinity. It leaves you feeling light, refreshed, and deeply nourished.

Reflection Juice feasting is far more than a nutritional practice; it is an invitation to reconnect with your body, mind, and spirit. Each glass of juice becomes a meditation, a reminder that you are choosing vitality, clarity, and renewal. When practiced with intention, juice feasting can reset your relationship with food, shift your energy, and cultivate mindfulness. Whether for a single day or a week-long feast, this ritual enables you to create sacred space for healing, insight, and lightness.

May every sip remind you that what you consume is not just fuel; it is medicine, prayer, and energy for the body, mind, and soul.

The Fruit Feasting Ritual

Fruits are one of nature's most vibrant gifts. They are alive with energy, full of life force, and designed to nourish and satisfy. Fruit feasting is a ritual that enables you to flood your system with vitamins, minerals, antioxidants, and hydration while delighting your senses. Unlike restrictive cleanses or diets, this practice encourages abundance, creativity, and joy, and each bite is a celebration of life.

> *"Your body communicates through cravings; your job is to understand the language."*

Why It Matters When you engage in a fruit feast, you are not just eating food; you are connecting with the natural rhythms of the Earth. Fruits, in their raw and colorful form, support detoxification, enhance energy levels, improve digestion, and elevate mood. They are a gift that nourishes both the physical body and the soul.

Healing Fruit Feasting Recipes Fruit feasting can be as simple or as creative as you like. The goal is to honor each fruit's unique properties and maximize their alkalizing, healing potential. While the body carefully regulates pH, alkaline-forming foods like fruits help reduce dietary acid load and support hydration, mineral balance, digestion, and the body's natural anti-inflammatory processes. To help you do this, I've included some of my favorite fruits along with alkaline recipes that have the power to energize your life.

Apple: Sweet Alkaline Apple Crisp Bowl

Why apple: Apples are rich in antioxidants and fiber, supporting liver detoxification and overall digestion. They are sweet, grounding, and versatile.

Ingredients:

2 large organic apples, diced
2 tbsp almond butter
1 tbsp chia seeds
1 tsp cinnamon
¼ cup soaked oats (optional)
Handful of crushed walnuts

Instructions:

1. Dice apples and toss with cinnamon.
2. Top with almond butter, chia seeds, and crushed walnuts.

3. Optional: mix in soaked oats for a creamy texture.
4. Serve chilled or slightly warmed.

This bowl screams comfort and energy in every bite.

Berries: Alkaline Berry Bliss Parfait

Why berries: Blueberries, strawberries, and raspberries are loaded with antioxidants and anti-inflammatory compounds that support brain health and reduce oxidative stress.

Ingredients:

½ cup blueberries
½ cup raspberries
½ cup strawberries, sliced
½ cup coconut yogurt (unsweetened)
1 tbsp hemp seeds
1 tsp maple syrup or raw agave

Instructions:

1. In a glass jar or bowl, layer coconut yogurt and berries alternately.
2. Sprinkle hemp seeds on top and drizzle with maple syrup.
3. Enjoy immediately or refrigerate for a chilled parfait.

This vibrant berry parfait is not only alkalizing but also visually nourishing. Its combination of colors, textures, and flavors energizes and satisfies.

Banana: Creamy Alkaline Banana Nice Cream

Why banana: Bananas are rich in potassium, support blood pressure regulation and aid digestion. They provide creamy sweetness naturally.

Ingredients:

2 frozen bananas
½ tsp vanilla extract
1 tbsp almond or cashew butter
1 tbsp cacao nibs

Instructions:

1. Blend frozen bananas with vanilla and nut butter until smooth.
2. Sprinkle cacao nibs on top.
3. Serve immediately as a soft-serve treat.

Banana nice cream is creamy, sweet, and satisfying without processed sugar. It is perfect for those craving dessert while staying fully alkaline.

Dates: Bliss Beauty Balls

Why dates: Dates are a natural energy booster, high in minerals and fiber, and support digestion and heart health.

Ingredients:

8 Medjool dates, pitted
¼ cup walnuts
1 tbsp cacao powder
Pinch of sea salt

Instructions:

1. Blend all ingredients in a food processor until sticky and uniform.
2. Roll into bite-sized balls.
3. Optional: roll in shredded coconut for extra texture.
4. Store in the fridge for a quick, energizing snack.

These bliss beauty balls are perfect for an alkalizing, grab-and-go snack that is both nutrient-dense and indulgent.

Figs: Fried Almond Butter and Fig Jelly Sandwich

Why figs: Figs are fiber-rich, support digestion and are high in antioxidants. This recipe is inspired by my Aunt Vaness. It's a fun, comforting, alkaline twist on a classic sandwich that I love to make for my guests.

Simple Fig Jelly Ingredients:

6 fresh figs, chopped
1 tbsp water
1 tsp lemon juice

Instructions:

1. Combine figs, water and lemon juice in a small saucepan.
2. Simmer over low heat for 10–15 minutes until figs break down.
3. Mash slightly and let cool.

Fried Almond Butter and Fig Jelly Sandwich Ingredients:

2 slices sprouted grain bread
2 tbsp almond butter
2 tbsp fig jelly
Coconut oil for frying

Instructions:

1. Spread almond butter on one slice of bread and fig jelly on the other.
2. Assemble the sandwich.
3. Heat a small amount of coconut oil in a pan and lightly fry the sandwich until golden brown on both sides.
4. Serve warm and slightly crispy.

This sandwich is indulgent, nostalgic, and delicious. It is a perfect fusion of comfort food and healing fruit energy.

Pineapple: Tropical Pineapple Fruit Bowl

Why pineapple: Pineapple contains bromelain, which aids digestion and has anti-inflammatory properties. Its bright, tropical flavor is energizing and hydrating.

Ingredients:

½ fresh pineapple, hollowed to create a bowl
½ cup pineapple chunks
½ cup mango, diced
½ cup papaya, diced
¼ cup shredded coconut
Handful of mint leaves

Instructions:

1. Use half the pineapple as a natural bowl.
2. Mix remaining pineapple chunks, mango, and papaya together.

3. Scoop mixture into pineapple bowl.
4. Sprinkle with coconut and garnish with mint leaves.
5. Serve chilled.

This tropical fruit bowl is perfect for summer brunches or a quick and refreshing energy boost.

Watermelon: Alkaline Watermelon Salad

Why watermelon: Watermelon is hydrating and rich in vitamins A and C. It cools the body, supports skin health, and replenishes electrolytes.

Ingredients:

2 cups watermelon cubes
½ cucumber, diced
¼ cup fresh mint leaves
1 tbsp lime juice
Pinch of sea salt

Instructions:

1. Toss watermelon and cucumber together in a bowl.
2. Add lime juice, mint leaves, and a pinch of sea salt.
3. Chill for 10 minutes before serving.

This watermelon salad is refreshingly sweet, hydrating, and alkalizing.

Fruit feasting is a ritual that celebrates abundance and vitality. By incorporating these fruits into your daily diet, you are feeding your body energy at the deepest level. Each fruit offers unique healing properties and can be prepared in ways that are both delicious and alkalizing.

This ritual is not just about nutrition, it's about honoring life itself. Fruits are gifts from the earth, vibrant with prana and a natural way to elevate your wellbeing. When you eat them mindfully, with gratitude and intention, every bite becomes a sacred experience.

Fruit feasting encourages creativity, mindfulness, and joy. It strengthens your connection to the natural world while cleansing, hydrating, and energizing your body. It is a ritual that nourishes not only your cells but also your soul.

The Vital Veggies Ritual

Vegetables are the cornerstone of vibrant health. They are alive with nutrients, antioxidants, and life force energy that help the body cleanse, repair, and thrive. This ritual is about embracing a rainbow of vegetables and exploring ways to incorporate them into your daily meals with intention, joy, and creativity. By honoring vegetables in your diet, you nourish your body at the deepest level, supporting vitality, longevity, and overall wellbeing.

> *"Your kitchen is your first wellness sanctuary."*

Why It Matters Eating a variety of vegetables ensures your body receives a wide spectrum of vitamins, minerals, and phytonutrients. Different colors and textures provide unique benefits, from supporting liver detoxification and gut health to reducing inflammation and protecting cells from oxidative stress. Vegetables can be enjoyed raw, lightly steamed, roasted, or blended into soups and smoothies. By preparing them thoughtfully, you elevate not only their nutrient potential but also your own sense of vitality.

Seven Vital Veggie Recipes These are some of the top healing vegetables and simple alkaline-focused recipes to make them an easy, enjoyable part of your daily routine.

Leafy Greens: Spinach and Avocado Power Salad

Why leafy greens: Spinach, Swiss chard, and other leafy greens are rich in vitamins A, C, K, and minerals like magnesium and iron. They support detoxification, overall health, and energy.

Ingredients:

2 cups fresh spinach
½ avocado, sliced
¼ cup walnuts, chopped
1 tbsp pumpkin seeds
1 tbsp lemon juice
1 tsp olive oil
Pinch of sea salt

Instructions:

1. Toss spinach with avocado, walnuts, and pumpkin seeds.
2. Drizzle with lemon juice and olive oil, and season with sea salt.
3. Serve immediately.

This simple salad is light, alkalizing, and nutrient-dense—a perfect start to any meal.

Cruciferous Vegetables: Roasted Broccoli and Cauliflower

Why cruciferous vegetables: Broccoli, cauliflower, and Brussels sprouts are high in fiber and cancer-fighting compounds, promoting gut health and reducing the risk of chronic diseases.

Ingredients:

1 cup broccoli florets
1 cup cauliflower florets
1 tbsp olive oil
1 tsp garlic powder
½ tsp paprika
Pinch of sea salt

Instructions:

1. Preheat oven to 400°F (200°C).
2. Toss broccoli and cauliflower with olive oil, garlic powder, paprika, and salt.
3. Roast for 20–25 minutes until tender and lightly golden.

Roasting enhances natural flavors while preserving the nutrients, making these cruciferous vegetables a satisfying and healthful dish.

Beets: Alkaline Beet and Carrot Salad

Why beets: Beets support liver function and detoxification while providing antioxidants and vitamins that help reduce inflammation.

Ingredients:

1 medium beet, peeled and grated

1 medium carrot, peeled and grated

1 tsp avocado oil

Juice of ½ lemon

Fresh parsley for garnish

Instructions:

1. Combine grated beet and carrot in a bowl.
2. Drizzle with avocado oil and lemon juice.
3. Toss gently and garnish with fresh parsley.

This version is light, alkalizing, and still deeply cleansing, while maintaining the vibrant flavors and nutrient density.

Carrots: Ginger Carrot Soup

Why carrots: Carrots are loaded with beta-carotene, which supports eye health, immunity, and overall vitality.

Ingredients:

4 large carrots, chopped

1 small zucchini, chopped

1 tsp fresh grated ginger

2 cups vegetable broth

½ tsp sea salt

Fresh thyme for garnish

Instructions:

1. In a saucepan, combine carrots, zucchini, ginger, and broth.
2. Simmer for 20 minutes until vegetables are soft.
3. Blend until smooth and season with salt.
4. Garnish with fresh thyme before serving.

This warming soup is alkalizing, soothing, and energizing for the body.

Bell Peppers: Stuffed Rainbow Peppers

Why bell peppers: High in vitamin C and antioxidants, bell peppers support immune function and skin health.

Ingredients:

2 red bell peppers, halved and deseeded
1 cup cooked quinoa
½ cup chopped spinach
¼ cup chopped walnuts
1 tsp olive oil
Pinch of sea salt and black pepper

Instructions:

1. Preheat oven to 375°F (190°C).
2. Mix quinoa, spinach, and walnuts together.
3. Stuff bell pepper halves with the mixture.
4. Drizzle with olive oil and bake for 15–20 minutes.

These stuffed peppers are colorful, nutrient-packed, and satisfying.

Zucchini: Zucchini Noodles with Pesto

Why zucchini: Zucchini is low in calories, hydrating, and full of vitamins and minerals.

Ingredients:

2 medium zucchinis, spiralized
2 tbsp walnut pesto (walnuts, basil, garlic, olive oil, lemon juice blended)
Pinch of sea salt

Instructions:

1. Toss zucchini noodles with walnut pesto until coated.
2. Serve raw for maximum alkalinity or lightly sauté for warmth.

This dish is light, fresh, and nourishing, a great way to enjoy raw or lightly cooked vegetables.

Stuffed Sweet Potato with Sautéed Mushrooms and Lemon-Roasted Asparagus

Why sweet potatoes: They are nutrient-dense, rich in fiber, vitamin A, and potassium, making them a satisfying base. Mushrooms add antioxidants and immune-supporting compounds, while asparagus brings vitamins, minerals, and natural diuretic properties. Together, this makes a vibrant, balanced, and alkalizing main dish.

Ingredients:

2 medium sweet potatoes
1 cup mushrooms, sliced (shiitake, cremini, or button)
1 tsp olive oil (for mushrooms)
1 bunch asparagus, trimmed
1 tsp olive oil (for asparagus)
1 tsp lemon juice
Pinch of sea salt
Optional: fresh herbs like parsley or thyme for garnish

Instructions:

1. Roast the sweet potatoes:
   - Preheat oven to 400°F (200°C).
   - Wash sweet potatoes and pierce with a fork a few times.
   - Place on a baking sheet and roast for 40–45 minutes, until tender when pierced with a fork.
2. Prepare the asparagus:
   - Toss trimmed asparagus with 1 tsp olive oil and a pinch of sea salt.
   - Place on the same baking sheet (or a separate one) and roast for 12–15 minutes until tender-crisp.
   - Drizzle with lemon juice before serving.
3. Sauté the mushrooms:
   - While the sweet potatoes are roasting, heat 1 tsp olive oil in a skillet over medium heat.
   - Add sliced mushrooms and sauté 5–7 minutes until soft and lightly browned.
   - Season with a pinch of sea salt and fresh herbs if desired.

4. Assemble the dish:
   - Once sweet potatoes are done, slice them open lengthwise and gently fluff the flesh with a fork.
   - Top each sweet potato with the sautéed mushrooms.
   - Serve alongside the lemon-roasted asparagus.

This dish is hearty, nourishing, and visually appealing—a perfect main course that balances complex carbohydrates, fiber, and micronutrients while keeping it light and alkalizing.

Reflection Vegetables are not just side dishes, they are medicine for the body and fuel for life. Incorporating a wide variety of colorful, nutrient-rich vegetables into your daily routine strengthens immunity, supports detoxification, and enhances overall energy levels. By engaging in this ritual mindfully, you honor the natural gifts of the earth while nourishing your body at the cellular level.

Vital veggies is a ritual that encourages abundance, creativity, and mindful eating. Every meal prepared with intention is a step toward vitality, resilience, and optimal wellbeing. When you prioritize vegetables in your diet, you are not only supporting your own health but also aligning with the natural rhythms of life itself.

The Superfoods Ritual

Superfoods are nature's most concentrated expressions of nourishment—whole, vibrant foods rich in vitamins, minerals, antioxidants, and life-supporting compounds. This ritual invites you to intentionally weave these powerful foods into your daily rhythms, transforming meals and drinks into acts of self-care, vitality, and devotion to your wellbeing. When you choose superfoods, you're not just eating, you're fueling your body, sharpening your mind, and activating your highest potential.

Throughout my own healing journey and in my work with clients, superfoods have played a foundational role in restoring energy, resilience, and clarity. I've also been deeply influenced by the teachings of my dear friend Anthony William, known as the Medical Medium, whose insights about healing foods and detoxification have supported my personal health and expanded the knowledge I share with others. While this ritual draws from a variety of holistic and plant-forward traditions, it honors the power of whole foods as intelligent allies in the body's natural healing process.

Why It Matters While there is no single definition of a "superfood," the foods in this section are widely recognized for their exceptional nutrient density and therapeutic potential. These ingredients appear throughout the recipes in this ritual and can be enjoyed regularly as part of a vibrant, balanced lifestyle:

Green Superfood Powders

- **Barley grass juice powder:** Rich in mineral salts that support detoxification and cellular hydration
- **Spirulina:** A powerful algae high in protein, antioxidants, and immune-supportive compounds
- **Moringa:** Nutrient-dense leaf powder known for supporting energy, inflammation balance, and blood sugar regulation

Seeds and Plant Proteins

- **Chia seeds:** Rich in fiber, omega-3s, and hydration-supporting properties
- **Hemp seeds:** A complete plant protein with essential fatty acids and minerals

Adaptogens and Functional Foods

- **Lucuma:** A naturally sweet Peruvian fruit powder that supports blood sugar balance.
- **Maca:** An adaptogenic root traditionally used to support energy, mood, and hormonal balance
- **Raw cacao:** Rich in magnesium, antioxidants, and mood-elevating compounds

Legumes and Ancient Staples

- **Lentils:** High in plant protein, fiber, and iron, supporting sustained energy
- **Quinoa:** A complete plant protein rich in minerals and amino acids

Fruits with Targeted Benefits

- **Wild blueberries:** Uniquely high in anthocyanins that support brain health and cellular repair
- **Dates:** Mineral-rich natural sweeteners that provide quick energy and digestive support
- **Bananas:** Nourishing for the nervous system and a key source of clean carbohydrates

Herbs, Roots, and Spices

- **Turmeric:** Supports inflammation balance and joint health
- **Ginger:** Aids digestion, circulation, and immune function
- **Cilantro:** Traditionally used to support detoxification

Sea Vegetables

- **Atlantic dulse:** Mineral-rich seaweed used to support detox and thyroid health

The Science Behind Superfoods Superfoods deliver a concentrated spectrum of nutrients that support the body at a cellular level. Rich in antioxidants, phytonutrients, fiber, and essential minerals, these foods help reduce inflammation, neutralize oxidative stress, support detoxification pathways, and nourish the brain, immune system, and nervous system. When incorporated consistently, superfoods can enhance energy production, cognitive function, and long-term vitality, helping the body operate with greater efficiency and resilience.

The recipes in this book are designed as a maintenance and lifestyle-support protocol, meant to nourish, energize, and support your overall well-being in a sustainable, everyday way. While many of the foods and principles are inspired by healing traditions and the work of the Medical Medium, these recipes are not intended to strictly follow Medical Medium protocols. For those navigating deep healing, chronic illness, or intensive detoxification, I highly recommend exploring and following the Medical Medium protocols directly, as they offer a more targeted and therapeutic approach. (Be sure to visit www.medicalmedium.com for more information about Anthony William and his teachings.)

How to Practice the Superfoods Ritual

1. **Set your intention:** Before preparing a superfood meal or snack, take a moment to connect with your intention. You might say silently or aloud, "I nourish my body with these foods to energize, strengthen, and heal."
2. **Prepare your superfoods:** Select one or more superfoods from the list in this section and incorporate them into a small meal, snack, or smoothie. Engage your senses as you prepare them—notice the color, aroma, and texture.

Superfood Recipes Incorporating superfoods into your daily meals provides the body with essential nutrients that support energy, immunity, and overall wellness. These recipes are simple, delicious, and designed to make nourishing your body feel fun, accessible, and sustainable.

Green Vitality Smoothie (Barley Grass Juice Powder + Spirulina + Moringa)

Ingredients:

1 tsp barley grass juice powder
½ tsp spirulina powder
½ tsp moringa powder
1 cup spinach
1 frozen banana
1 cup coconut water

Instructions:

1. Combine all ingredients in a high-speed blender.
2. Blend until smooth and creamy.
3. Sip slowly, savoring the deep green vitality flowing through you.

Chia Seed Pudding with Berries

Ingredients:

3 tbsp chia seeds

1 cup almond milk or other plant-based milk

½ tsp vanilla extract

1 tsp lucuma powder

Fresh berries for topping

Instructions:

1. Mix chia seeds, plant-based milk, vanilla, and lucuma powder in a bowl.
2. Refrigerate for at least two hours or overnight.
3. Top with fresh berries before serving. Enjoy each bite mindfully.

High-Energy Salad with Quinoa and Lentils

Ingredients:

2 cups mixed leafy greens

1 tbsp hemp seeds

½ avocado, sliced

½ cup cooked quinoa

½ cup cooked lentils

1 tsp olive oil

Juice of ½ lemon

Instructions:

1. Combine leafy greens, avocado, quinoa, lentils, and hemp seeds in a bowl.
2. Drizzle with olive oil and lemon juice.
3. Toss gently and enjoy the hearty, nutrient-dense, and vibrant flavors.

Snickers Date Bark

Ingredients:

1 cup medjool dates, pitted
½ cup walnuts
2 tbsp raw cacao powder
2 tbsp natural almond butter
Pinch of sea salt
Optional: 1 tsp coconut oil

Instructions:

1. Blend dates, almond butter, cacao powder, and coconut oil (if using) in a food processor until smooth.
2. Roughly chop walnuts and fold into the mixture.
3. Spread the mixture onto a parchment-lined tray about ½ inch thick.
4. Chill in the refrigerator for 30–45 minutes until firm.
5. Cut into squares or rectangles and enjoy a date bark that tastes like a Snickers bar.

Heavy Metal Detox Smoothie (Anthony William)

Ingredients:

2 bananas
2 cups frozen or fresh wild blueberries (or 2 oz pure wild blueberry juice, or 2 tbsp pure wild blueberry powder)
1 cup tightly packed fresh cilantro
1 tsp barley grass juice powder
1 tsp spirulina
1 tbsp Atlantic dulse (or 2 dropperfuls Atlantic dulse liquid)
Juice of 1 orange
½ to 1 cup water, coconut water, or additional fresh-squeezed orange juice (optional, to adjust consistency)

Instructions:

1. Combine all ingredients in a high-speed blender.
2. Blend until smooth. Add water, coconut water, or additional juice if a thinner consistency is desired.
3. Serve immediately.

Wild blueberries are recommended for their unique detoxifying phytonutrients, which support heavy metal elimination and oxidative repair.

Golden Glow Turmeric Latte

Ingredients:

1 cup unsweetened almond milk
½ tsp turmeric powder
¼ tsp cinnamon
½ tsp ginger powder or fresh grated ginger
1 tsp maple syrup or honey
Pinch of black pepper

Instructions:

1. Heat almond milk gently on the stove.
2. Whisk in turmeric, cinnamon, ginger, sweetener, and black pepper until smooth.
3. Pour into a mug and enjoy as a warming, gut-soothing beverage.

Blueberry Brain Smoothie

Ingredients:

½ avocado
1 cup frozen blueberries
1 cup spinach
1 tbsp hemp seeds
1 cup oat milk or almond milk
½ tsp maca powder (optional)

Instructions:

1. Blend all ingredients in a high-speed blender until creamy.
2. Sip mindfully to support brain function, energy, and mental clarity.

By adding these recipes into your weekly meals, you are giving your body the tools it needs to function optimally. Each recipe is a playful, nourishing ritual that reminds you that self-care can be fun, vibrant, and transformational. As you practice, notice how your body feels, how your energy flows, and how your mind sharpens; each bite and sip is an act of self-love and empowerment.

The Sustainable Supplements Ritual

Supplements can help fill nutrient gaps, support energy, immunity, and overall wellbeing. This ritual invites you to mindfully incorporate essential supplements into your daily routine, prioritizing clean, plant-based, and environmentally conscious options. By choosing wisely, you honor both your body and the planet.

Why It Matters Even with a nutrient-rich diet, modern lifestyles, stress, and soil depletion can leave gaps in essential vitamins and minerals. Supplementing sustainably ensures your body receives the nutrients it needs for optimal health without harming the environment.

How to Practice the Sustainable Supplements Ritual

1. **Set your intention:** Before taking supplements, focus on your purpose: "I nourish my body with pure, conscious nutrition to thrive, heal, and flourish."
2. **Choose mindfully:** Look for:
   - Plant-based or vegan options
   - Non-GMO and ethically sourced ingredients
   - Minimal processing to preserve potency
   - Eco-friendly packaging

Top 10 Supplements Most People Commonly Need

- Vitamin D3: Supports bone health, immunity, and mood
- Vitamin B12: Essential for energy, nerve health, and red blood cells, especially for those on plant-based diets
- Magnesium: Supports muscle function, sleep, stress management, and heart health
- Omega-3 (vegan or fish-based): Supports brain, heart, and eye health
- Probiotics: Promote gut health, digestion, and immune function
- Vitamin C: Powerful antioxidant that supports immunity, skin, and collagen production
- Zinc: Supports immune function, wound healing, and hormone balance
- Iron (plant-based or gentle form): Essential for energy, blood health, and oxygen transport
- Iodine: Supports thyroid function and metabolism
- Adaptogenic herbs (ashwagandha, rhodiola, or medicinal mushrooms): Support stress resilience, energy, and hormonal balance

By intentionally incorporating these supplements into your routine, you ensure your body receives the nutrients it needs to thrive. Each supplement becomes a conscious act of self-care, supporting vitality, mental clarity and overall resilience. Sustainable supplementation is a way to honor yourself while caring for the environment, creating balance and harmony in your daily wellness practice.

The Mindful Hydration Rituals

Water is life. Yet in the modern world, we often overlook its transformative power. Beyond quenching thirst, mindful hydration can revitalize the body, support digestion, flush toxins, and elevate energy. In this ritual, I invite you to approach water not as a mundane necessity, but as a sacred daily practice, an opportunity to nourish, cleanse, and reconnect with your body's natural rhythms.

The Power of Water Our bodies are composed of approximately 60% water, and every cell depends on it to function optimally. Proper hydration supports digestion, circulation, cognitive clarity, and hormone regulation. Beyond these essentials, water can become a vessel for intention and vitality. By infusing water with nutrient-rich ingredients, we amplify its healing potential.

"Hydration is a love language."

Hydration is not just about quantity, it's about quality, intention, and rhythm. Mindful hydration turns a simple act into a holistic ritual that nurtures both body and mind. When approached with consciousness, water becomes a conduit for cleansing, energy restoration, and inner balance.

How to Practice Mindful Hydration

1. **Set your intention:** Before drinking, pause for a moment and take a deep breath. Set an intention for your hydration practice, such as "With each sip, I nourish my body, clear my mind, and restore my energy."
2. **Choose clean water:** Filtered or spring water is ideal. Avoid plastics when possible and opt for glass or stainless steel bottles. This ensures purity and supports environmental sustainability.
3. **Drink slowly and consciously:** Sip mindfully, noticing the temperature, texture, and how your body feels with each drink. Drinking too quickly can reduce absorption and overwhelm the digestive system.
4. **Time your hydration:** Spread water intake throughout the day. Begin with a glass on waking to rehydrate after sleep and enjoy a glass 30 minutes before meals to support digestion.

Gut-Nourishing Waters Infusing water with healing ingredients enhances hydration and supports the gut, the root of immunity and vitality. This section describes several recipes that combine alkalizing, detoxifying, and digestive-boosting properties.

Cucumber + Mint + Lemon Water

Ingredients:
½ cucumber, sliced thin
6–8 fresh mint leaves
½ lemon, thinly sliced
1 liter filtered water

Instructions:
1. Add cucumber, mint, and lemon slices to a pitcher of water.
2. Let infuse for one to two hours in the fridge.
3. Sip throughout the day to stay hydrated and support digestion.

Ginger + Lemon + Turmeric Water

Ingredients:
1-inch fresh ginger, sliced
½ lemon, juiced
½ tsp turmeric powder or 1-inch turmeric root, sliced
1 liter filtered water

Instructions:
1. Add ginger, turmeric, and lemon to water.
2. Let infuse for 30–60 minutes.
3. Drink slowly to reduce inflammation and support gut health.

Apple + Cinnamon + Clove Water

Ingredients:
½ organic apple, sliced
1 cinnamon stick
3–4 whole cloves
1 liter filtered water

Instructions:

1. Combine ingredients in a glass pitcher.
2. Let infuse for one to two hours.
3. Enjoy for gentle blood sugar balance and digestive support.

Pineapple + Basil + Lime Water

Ingredients:

½ cup pineapple chunks
4–5 fresh basil leaves
½ lime, sliced
1 liter filtered water

Instructions:

1. Add all ingredients to water.
2. Infuse for one to two hours.
3. Sip to support digestion, reduce bloating, and encourage hydration.

Watermelon + Mint + Chia Seed Water

Ingredients:

1 cup watermelon cubes
6–8 fresh mint leaves
1 tsp chia seeds
1 liter filtered water

Instructions:

1. Add watermelon, mint, and chia seeds to water.
2. Allow to sit for 30 minutes so chia seeds expand.
3. Drink slowly to hydrate and nourish the gut while replenishing electrolytes.

Aloe Vera + Cucumber + Lemon Water

Ingredients:
2 tbsp fresh aloe vera gel
½ cucumber, sliced
½ lemon, sliced
1 liter filtered water

Instructions:

1. Combine all ingredients in a pitcher.
2. Chill for one hour before sipping.
3. Drink to support digestion, soothe the gut lining, and promote hydration.

Okra Water

Ingredients:
2–3 fresh okra pods, sliced
½ lemon, sliced
1 liter filtered water

Instructions:

1. Add sliced okra and lemon to a pitcher of water.
2. Let infuse for six to eight hours in the fridge for optimal gut-nourishing benefits.
3. Sip throughout the day to support digestion, improve gut lining, and enhance nutrient absorption.

Making Hydration a Ritual Mindful hydration is more than just drinking water, it's about honoring your body and creating a moment of presence. To fully embrace this ritual, do the following:

- **Use a beautiful vessel:** Choose a glass bottle or jar that brings you joy. The visual appeal encourages regular sipping.

- **Create a routine:** Pair your water practice with meditation, journaling, or a short breathwork session to deepen the ritual.
- **Infuse with gratitude:** With each sip, silently thank your body for its resilience and your mind for its clarity.

By adopting mindful hydration, you transform a simple daily necessity into a sacred practice. The waters you drink not only support physical health but also promote mental clarity, emotional balance, and energetic vitality. Infused with nutrient-rich ingredients, these gut-nourishing waters become a tool for restoration and renewal, helping you cultivate a deeper connection to your body and its innate intelligence.

As you sip your water, remember that every drop nourishes, heals, and energizes. Through conscious hydration, you honor life itself, one mindful sip at a time.

Optional Exploration: Nurturing Your Nutritional Wellbeing

Cleanse to Heal, Anthony William. A comprehensive guide to using natural foods and detox protocols to restore health and vitality.

Colorful Home Cooking, Gabrielle Reyes. Celebrates plant-based eating with joyful, flavor-packed recipes that nourish body and spirit.

PlantYou, Carleigh Bodrug. Simplifies plant-based cooking with practical recipes and sustainable meal planning for everyday life.

It's All About Plantz & Mushroomz, Todd Anderson. Encourages nutrient-rich eating rooted in plant-based principles for long-term wellness.

Chris Beat Cancer, Chris Wark. Shares one man's healing journey and evidence-based nutrition strategies for disease prevention.

How Not to Die, Michael Greger, MD. Explores the link between diet and longevity, offering practical nutrition science for optimal health.

JoyFull, Radhi Devlukia-Shetty. Combines Ayurvedic wisdom and mindful nourishment to bring balance and bliss to every meal.

These books serve as companions to your nutritional journey. Some provide practical recipes, others evidence-based strategies, and some center culture, identity, and mindfulness. Open them when you feel drawn and allow your intuition to guide which messages resonate most deeply. Remember, your body already knows how to thrive; these resources simply help you connect with and amplify that innate wisdom.

Reference

Kan, J., Wu, F., Wang, F., Zheng, J., Cheng, J., Li, Y., Yang, Y., & Du, J. (2022). Phytonutrients: Sources, bioavailability, interaction with gut microbiota, and their impacts on human health. *Frontiers in Nutrition*, *9*, 960309. 10.3389/fnut.2022.960309.

5 Physical Wellbeing

Tohamina / Freepik

Your Body Is Your Sacred Temple and Your Home Is Your Sacred Space

There comes a moment when you realize your body is not an obstacle to overcome; it's a sacred vessel carrying you through.

I remember the first time I truly felt at home in my body. It wasn't during one of my best track meets or when I graduated with honors, or even when I looked in the mirror and liked what I saw. It was a quiet, ordinary morning. The sun was shining on me through my window, and I had just finished a gentle yoga flow. My breath slowed, my body softened, and suddenly I could feel the aliveness in every cell of my body. My heart was beating steadily. My lungs were expanding and contracting, giving me breath. My blood was moving, warm and constant.

In that moment, I realized something so simple and yet so profound: My body wasn't something to conquer, perfect, or control. It was already whole. Already sacred.

And as I looked around my room, bathed in golden light, I noticed something else: My home, too, was holding me. The calm of uncluttered space, a soft blanket gently providing me warmth, the sacred order of a sanctuary. Just as my body was a vessel for my soul, my home was a vessel for my body. Both were sacred, and both deserved care.

For most of my life, I hadn't seen them this way. My body was a project to fix. My home was a place to crash. But in that morning stillness, I saw the truth: The way we live in our bodies and the way we live in our homes are reflections of each other. When my home feels chaotic, my body carries that weight. When my body feels neglected, my home mirrors it back. Healing, I realized, requires tending to both.

The Innocence and Early Messages

When I think back to my earliest memories, I remember moments of pure innocence with my body. Running barefoot in the grass. Laughing as I spun in circles until I collapsed dizzy on the ground. Stretching my arms toward the sky without a thought about how I looked, only how free I felt.

But alongside those experiences of freedom, there were other realities, too. My childhood home didn't always feel safe. There was love, yes, but there was also emotional turmoil. Raised voices. Arguments. An energy that kept my nervous system on edge. Inside those walls, I often felt like I had to shrink, to protect myself, to run, for release.

And so I did run. Out into the yard. Into sports. Into books and imagination. My body, even when I pushed it hard, felt safer than my home. Movement became my escape. Fresh air became my comfort. The wide-open sky became my sanctuary.

Looking back, I see how deeply this shaped me. When your home doesn't feel safe, you learn to hold everything inside. Your body becomes both a shield and storage. You carry what you can't release. And even if the house itself is still standing, the foundation of safety is cracked.

That early experience planted seeds I didn't yet understand. Seeds of vigilance. Seeds of striving. Seeds of believing that maybe if I perfected my body, maybe if I achieved enough, maybe then I'd feel safe, even if home wasn't.

The Pursuit of Perfection

When I became an athlete, that seed of striving bloomed into full force. My body became my instrument, my tool, my ticket to a better life. On the outside, people admired my discipline, my strength, my achievements. And there's no denying that there was pride and joy in being able to perform at such a high level.

But beneath the surface, something more complicated was happening.

I pushed my body hard, often harder than I should have. Training when I was exhausted. Ignoring pain. Restricting rest because I thought rest was weakness. My relationship with food wasn't always about nourishment; sometimes it was about control. My relationship with movement wasn't always about joy; sometimes it was about proving myself.

The body became a battlefield. A place of striving, of constant demand. And even when I reached milestones, the satisfaction didn't last. There was always another record to chase, another level of performance to reach.

And my home during that time? It often reflected my inner state. Sometimes neat and orderly, but often cluttered with gear, scattered clothes, and the restless energy of a body that never stopped. My space wasn't a sanctuary; it was storage. A place to recover just enough to push again.

Looking back, I can see how disconnected I was. I wasn't listening to my body's wisdom; I was silencing it. My body whispered through little aches and fatigue, but I brushed it off. When the whispers grew louder into pain and injury, I pushed harder. I thought strength meant overriding my body. Now I know true strength is learning to listen.

Breaking Point

The body will always speak, and if we don't listen to its whispers, it will eventually scream.

My breaking point came after a season of injuries, stress, and exhaustion. On the outside, I still looked strong. I still smiled, still showed up, still pushed through. But on the inside, my body was crumbling under the weight of all I was asking it to carry.

One night, after a long day of training, I collapsed into bed and felt tears spill down my cheeks. My muscles ached, but it wasn't just physical pain. It was grief. Grief for how I had treated my body. Grief for how I had confused performance with worth. Grief for how I had ignored the signals that something had to change. I knew my back wasn't fully healed the first time I tried to return to the track.

And I noticed something else, too: The room around me felt heavy. Clothes piled in corners. Papers scattered on the desk. Dust collecting on shelves. My apartment wasn't soothing me; it was suffocating me. The lack of care I had shown my body was mirrored in my space. Both were crying out for love.

In that quiet darkness, I placed my hand on my heart. For the first time in years, I didn't ask my body to do more. I didn't criticize it. I didn't demand perfection. I simply said, "I'm sorry. Thank you. I promise to do better."

It may sound simple, but those words were the beginning of everything shifting. That night was a turning point. A sacred moment when I stopped seeing my body as an enemy to fight and began seeing it as a partner to honor. And slowly, I realized the same had to be true for my home.

Turning Toward Healing

Healing didn't happen overnight. It was, and still is, a process, a practice, a daily choice.

At first, I didn't know what it meant to treat my body with compassion instead of criticism. I had to unlearn years of conditioning. I had to catch myself when I started to judge. I had to pause when I wanted to push too far. I had to remind myself that rest was not weakness, that nourishment was not indulgence, that I deserved to be nurtured.

And alongside body rituals, I began home rituals, too:

- Placing my hand on my heart in gratitude before I even got out of bed
- Moving my body in ways that felt joyful, not just efficient
- Choosing food not only for fuel but for vibrancy and delight
- Clearing clutter and creating corners of my home that felt like a sanctuary
- Opening windows for fresh air, lighting candles, inviting softness into my space
- Creating evening rituals that honored sleep as sacred reset
- Learning to say no when my body whispered for rest, and yes when my home whispered for peace

> *"Healing the body is not just about recovery from pain, but about returning to presence and reclaiming the energy and vitality that has always belonged to you."*

Each choice was like a new conversation with my body. Each act of self-care was like an offering to the highest version of myself.

Science Meets Spirit

The more I honored my body and my home, the more I noticed not just spiritual shifts, but tangible, physical ones. My energy stabilized. My stress lowered. My sleep deepened.

Research affirms what I was experiencing. Studies in the *Journal of Health Psychology* (Ramseyer Winter et al., 2019) show that practicing body appreciation leads to reduced stress, improved resilience, and even stronger immune function. And studies on environment and wellbeing reveal that cluttered or chaotic homes can increase cortisol (the stress hormone), while clean, calm environments can enhance mood, creativity, and focus.

Movement, rest, nourishment, and environment are not just "healthy habits"; they are medicine for the nervous system, for the heart, for the soul.

But beyond the science, there's something deeper. When you honor your body and your home, you're not just improving health metrics. You're awakening to the miracle of being alive and held. Every breath becomes a gift. Every meal becomes communion. Every corner of your home becomes a sanctuary.

Reflection and Invitation

Looking back now, I see how my healing journey with my body mirrors my healing journey with my home. In both, I had to let go of the illusion of control. In both, I had to stop chasing external validation. In both, I had to remember what was true all along: Wholeness was never outside of me; it was always within and around.

> *"Trust your body's wisdom. Every ache, every stretch, every breath is a message guiding you toward balance and renewal."*

Healing your relationship with your body is healing your relationship with life itself. Healing your relationship with your home is creating the conditions for that life to flourish. Because your body is the place where life happens. And your home is the sacred space that holds it all.

Every laugh, every tear, every hug, every dance, every dream; they all move through your body and your home.

The Invitation

And so, I invite us to consider these questions:

- What if our bodies and our homes were never meant to be perfect? What if they were simply meant to be honored?
- What if every stretch, every breath, every heartbeat, and every sacred corner of our homes is a reminder that we are alive right now, and that is enough?
- What if instead of controlling, we chose connecting?
- What if instead of punishing, we chose partnering?
- What if instead of criticizing, we chose celebrating?

When we treat our bodies as sacred temples and our homes as sacred spaces, everything shifts. We move with more ease. We eat with more gratitude. We rest with more intention. We live with more joy.

Our bodies are not obstacles. They are offerings.

Our homes are not burdens. They are blessings.

Neither are cages to confine us; they are sacred vessels carrying us through this life.

> *"Physical wellbeing begins when you give yourself permission to honor your body's rhythms—to rest when you're tired, to move when you're inspired, to listen when it whispers."*

Seven Sacred Physical Wellbeing Rituals

Your physical body is not something to fix or control; it is something to honor, listen to, and partner with. These seven sacred physical wellbeing rituals are invitations to return to your body with reverence, transforming everyday movements into practices that nourish vitality, presence, and lasting self-trust.

The Body Gratitude Ritual: Your Body Is Your Sacred Temple

Your body is the vessel through which you experience life—your sacred temple. But, many of us wake up already at war with our bodies. We criticize the way we look in the mirror, wish we were different, or ignore our body's signals until exhaustion or illness forces us to pay attention. This ritual invites you to begin each day with a conscious shift: moving from criticism to compassion, from disconnection to gratitude.

A study published in *Body Image* found that higher levels of self-compassion were associated with greater body satisfaction and reduced body image concerns (Wasylkiw et al., 2012). When you rise in the morning, before the world pulls you into its noise, place your hand on your heart or belly and whisper, "Thank you, body, for carrying me." Feel the warmth of your hand, the rhythm of your breath, and the steady beat of your heart. This simple gesture reminds you that your body has been faithfully serving you since the day you were born. Every scar, curve, and stretch mark is part of your sacred story.

But this ritual is not just about affirmations; it's about shifting your relationship with your body over time. Instead of approaching your body with judgment, you begin to cultivate reverence. Each morning becomes an opportunity to reset: "How can I honor this body today?" Maybe it's through nourishing food, gentle stretching, or simply resting when you need it.

Client Story: Alana's Journey to Body Gratitude

Alana, a 42-year-old mother of three, came to me feeling disconnected from her body. After years of dieting and critical self-talk, she described her mornings as "a battle with the mirror." Even when she achieved her "goal weight," she admitted she never felt enough.

We introduced the Body Gratitude Ritual into her mornings. At first, it felt awkward to her; placing her hand on her heart and whispering gratitude seemed forced. She said, "I felt silly talking to myself like that." But I encouraged her to stay with it, even if the words didn't feel fully true yet.

Within three weeks, something shifted. She began noticing how her body supported her daily: carrying groceries, hugging her children, even healing from old injuries. Instead of criticizing her belly, she thanked it for carrying life. Instead of resenting her wrinkles, she honored them as marks of wisdom.

Months later, Alana shared that this ritual had transformed her mornings. "I no longer start my day hating my body," she said. "Now, I start with gratitude. And when I care for myself—whether it's eating better or moving more—it comes from love, not punishment."

Alana's story reflects what research confirms: When we practice body gratitude, behaviors naturally align with health and wellbeing, because they come from compassion rather than shame.

Why It Works This ritual rewires your self-perception. By practicing daily gratitude and self-affirmation, you shift from negative self-talk (which increases cortisol and stress) toward self-compassion (which lowers stress and boosts resilience). Over time, this creates not only greater body satisfaction but also healthier long-term habits.

Your body is your home. When you treat it as sacred, everything changes. Begin each day by honoring your temple, and you'll carry that energy of love and reverence throughout your life.

The Dancing Daily Ritual

Movement is medicine, and dance is one of the most joyful, liberating forms of it. Unlike structured exercise, dance doesn't demand equipment, perfect technique, or even a set time. All it asks is that you let music guide you. Whether it's two minutes of swaying while your morning coffee brews or a full session of movement in your living room, dancing shakes off stagnant energy and reconnects you to joy.

Whether you're moving to a rhythm you love or participating in structured dance classes, science shows that dance matters. An evidence-based review of dozens of controlled research studies indicates that regular dance interventions have measurable positive effects on emotional regulation, mental health, and overall wellbeing (Koch et al., 2019).

Dancing daily is more than physical activity—it's an emotional release. Your body stores stress and unprocessed emotions, and through movement, you allow them to surface and dissolve. Think of dance as a reset button; each spin, sway, or stomp becomes a way to shake loose what no longer serves you.

Client Story: Tina's Return to Joy

Tina, a 29-year-old creative professional, came to me feeling burned out. She described her life as "all deadlines, no fun." When asked what brought her joy as a child, she instantly said, "Dancing." She had danced freely in her bedroom as a teenager but stopped after college when "real life" got in the way.

I challenged Tina to reintroduce daily dance; just one song in the morning. At first, she resisted. "I felt ridiculous," she admitted.

(continued)

(*continued*)

But within a week, she noticed something shifting. She laughed at herself in the mirror, her mood lifted before work, and her creative blocks began to ease.

Three months later, Tina reported she was "hooked." Dancing had become her moving meditation. She used it to process stress, celebrate victories, and reconnect with her inner child. "When I dance, I remember who I am," she said. "It's like therapy without words."

Her coworkers even noticed she seemed lighter, more energetic, and more present. Dance had reignited her spark.

Why It Works Dance is unique because it combines movement, music, and emotion. Unlike running or lifting weights, it is inherently expressive. By surrendering to rhythm, you bypass the analytical mind and drop into flow, a state where time fades and joy emerges.

From a physiological perspective, dance increases endorphins, balances the nervous system, and improves cardiovascular health. From a psychological perspective, it enhances mood, reduces anxiety, and fosters self-expression. And from a spiritual perspective, dance is prayer in motion—a way to commune with life itself.

Even two minutes a day can shift your energy. The more you practice, the more you'll discover that dance is not just exercise but a daily ritual of liberation.

The Dry Brushing Ritual

Dry brushing is a simple yet powerful ritual that awakens the body and mind. Using a natural bristle brush, you gently sweep your skin in circular motions toward the heart before showering. On the surface, this exfoliates dead skin, leaving it radiant. But beneath the skin, something deeper happens: Circulation increases, the lymphatic system is stimulated, and energy begins to flow more freely.

Dry brushing has long been used in traditional wellness systems as a ritual of renewal and self-care. While it is often described as supporting lymphatic flow or detoxification, current scientific evidence does not show that dry brushing directly enhances lymphatic drainage or removes toxins from the body.

What *is* well supported is the experiential impact of the practice: dry brushing exfoliates the skin and provides rhythmic sensory stimulation, which many people experience as energizing and refreshing.

This ritual becomes even more powerful when paired with visualization. As you brush, imagine sweeping away stress, negativity, or fatigue. Each stroke becomes a symbolic cleansing, preparing you to step into the shower lighter, clearer, and renewed.

Client Story: Rachel's Morning Reset

Rachel, a 37-year-old entrepreneur, often described her mornings as chaotic. Between managing her team and caring for her two kids, she said she woke up already "two steps behind." She wanted a ritual that would ground her before diving into the day.

We introduced dry brushing as a mindful morning practice. The first week, Rachel admitted she almost gave up; it felt too simple to make a difference. But by the second week, she noticed a shift: "It's like I shed the sleepiness and anxiety with every brush stroke."

She began pairing the ritual with affirmations: as she brushed her arms, she said, "I release stress." As she brushed her legs, she whispered, "I step forward with confidence." Over time, dry brushing became her morning reset. She described it as "coffee for the soul" energizing, cleansing, and centering.

Six months later, Rachel shared that her skin felt healthier, but more important, her mornings felt sacred. "I don't rush into my day anymore," she said. "I begin with intention and clarity."

Why It Works Physiologically, dry brushing supports circulation and lymphatic drainage, helping the body detoxify naturally. Psychologically, it creates a pause—a mindful moment where you connect with your body before being pulled into external demands. Spiritually, it becomes a ritual of release, clearing stagnant energy so you can move through your day renewed.

The beauty lies in its simplicity. Just five minutes before your shower can shift your energy, improve your skin, and anchor your mornings in ritual.

The Yoga and Mobility Ritual

Yoga and mobility are about more than flexibility; they are practices of freedom. With just 10–20 minutes a day, you can soften tight muscles, release stored tension, and bring fluidity back into your joints. These movements are not only physical; they unravel stress and reconnect you with breath, presence, and inner calm.

Harvard Medical School (2018) reports that yoga reduces stress hormones while increasing gamma-aminobutyric acid, a neurotransmitter that calms the nervous system and relieves anxiety. This biochemical effect explains why even short sessions leave you feeling grounded and centered.

By focusing on the hips, spine, and shoulders—the body's storage lockers for tension—you open up not only physical space but also emotional release. Many people describe feeling lighter and more spacious after just a few poses.

Client Story: David's Healing Through Mobility

David, a 50-year-old executive, came to me after years of chronic back pain. He admitted he had ignored his body while climbing the corporate ladder. "I thought yoga was for flexible people, not for me," he said. But he was willing to try.

We started with gentle mobility drills; cat-cows, seated twists, hip openers, and short yoga flows. At first, David was frustrated. He struggled to touch his toes and felt stiff. But I encouraged him to focus on breath, not performance.

Within two months, his back pain decreased significantly. Even more surprising to him was the mental shift. "I handle stress so much better now. It's like the tension doesn't stick the way it used to." Yoga had become his refuge.

Now, David practices 15 minutes of yoga and mobility daily before work. "It's not just about pain relief anymore," he said. "It's about starting my day with clarity and peace."

Why It Works Yoga and mobility practices combine physical release with neurological and emotional benefits. They restore range of motion, improve posture, and prevent injuries, while also calming the nervous system. Breath-centered movement anchors you in the present moment, transforming the mat into a sanctuary of renewal.

This ritual reminds you that you don't have to carry tension all day. You can release it—one stretch, one breath, one moment at a time.

> *"Every step you take with awareness, every stretch you hold with compassion, every breath you deepen with intention; these are rituals of physical wellbeing."*

A Mile a Day Ritual

Walking, jogging, or running a mile each day may sound simple, but this ritual carries incredible benefits for your body, mind, and spirit. One mile isn't about competition or hitting a certain pace; it's about consistency and intention. Each step becomes an act of devotion, a moving meditation where you reconnect with yourself and the world around you.

Research by Oppezzo and Schwartz found that walking can significantly enhance creative thinking compared to sitting, with participants generating up to 60% more creative ideas while walking (Oppezzo & Schwartz, 2014). Walking has also been widely associated with reduced anxiety, improved cardiovascular health, and enhanced mood, benefits linked to gentle aerobic movement and neurochemical changes that support emotional wellbeing.

When practiced daily, walking becomes more than exercise; it becomes a grounding ritual; a simple, accessible practice that integrates movement, presence, and mindful awareness.

Your daily mile can take many forms: a brisk walk outdoors, a jog at sunrise, or a treadmill session paired with reflection. The key is presence. Treat each step as sacred. Inhale strength, exhale stress. Let your body set the rhythm, and your breath become the mantra.

Client Story: Mark's Daily Reset

Mark, a 46-year-old graphic designer, came to me overwhelmed by stress. His work kept him indoors for long hours, and he admitted to barely moving some days. "I feel stuck—mentally and physically," he said.

I suggested the "mile-a-day" ritual. Mark resisted at first. "What difference can one mile make?" But he agreed to try.

The first week, Mark walked slowly around his neighborhood after dinner. He noticed small things he had been missing—children playing, the way the sunset painted the sky, the rhythm of his own breath. By the third week, he felt calmer, less reactive at work, and even more creative in his projects.

Three months later, Mark had turned his mile into a cherished ritual. Sometimes he walked in silence; other times, he listened to audiobooks or uplifting music. "It's my daily reset button," he told me. "Even on the hardest days, I know I can walk it off—literally."

The ripple effects were powerful: he lost weight, slept better, and noticed fewer stress-related headaches. But most important, he said, "I feel alive again."

Why It Works Walking is deceptively powerful. It lowers cortisol, improves circulation, and nourishes creativity by engaging the brain in a state of flow. Psychologically, it creates a rhythm of release—each step letting go of stress, each breath inviting clarity. Spiritually, it grounds you in the present moment and connects you to the earth beneath your feet.

One mile may be short in distance, but its impact accumulates. Over time, this ritual teaches you that small, consistent steps lead to big transformation.

Cardio and Strength Training Ritual

Balancing cardiovascular exercise with strength training creates a foundation for vitality that supports you for life. Cardio strengthens your heart and lungs, regulating mood and boosting endurance. Strength training builds lean muscle, protects bone density, and empowers you with resilience. Together, they create a holistic approach to fitness; not punishment, but empowerment.

According to the Mayo Clinic (2022), strength training not only prevents muscle loss and osteoporosis but also improves confidence and reduces the risk of chronic illnesses like diabetes and heart disease. Cardiovascular activity, however, has been shown to elevate mood, regulate blood pressure, and increase longevity.

The key to this ritual is variety and joy. Cardio doesn't have to mean hours on a treadmill; it could be cycling, dancing, hiking, or swimming. Strength training doesn't require heavy weights; bodyweight movements like squats, planks, or push-ups can be just as effective. The focus isn't on perfection but on how alive and strong you feel afterward.

Client Story: Jasmine's Empowerment Through Strength

Jasmine, a 35-year-old teacher, had always associated exercise with punishment. Growing up, she remembered gym teachers scolding her and endless diets tied to workouts. "I thought of fitness as something I had to do, not something I wanted to do," she told me.

(*continued*)

(*continued*)

We reframed her relationship with movement by creating a ritual of alternating cardio and strength training. Three days a week, she danced to her favorite playlists for cardio. Two days a week, she practiced strength circuits using bodyweight and resistance bands.

At first, she doubted herself. "I didn't think I was strong enough." But over time, she surprised herself—holding planks longer, doing more push-ups, and noticing her stamina increase. "For the first time, I don't dread workouts," Jasmine said. "I feel proud, powerful, even joyful."

The shift wasn't just physical. Jasmine reported more confidence in her classroom, more patience with her students, and even better sleep. Movement had become a form of self-respect rather than punishment.

Why It Works Cardio and strength training together offer a balanced prescription for health. Cardio strengthens the cardiovascular system and enhances mood through endorphins. Strength training builds physical and emotional resilience by reminding you of your capacity. Psychologically, alternating between the two prevents burnout and keeps exercise fun.

Spiritually, this ritual teaches balance: the rhythm of heart-pumping cardio and the grounding of strength. It's a reminder that you are both dynamic and steady, resilient and adaptable.

Your Sanctuary Ritual

The spaces you live in shape your health more than you may realize. When your home is filled with toxins, clutter, or harsh energy, it can quietly drain your vitality. By transforming your home into a sanctuary, you create an environment that nourishes your body, calms your mind, and uplifts your spirit.

Detoxification begins with what we bring into our homes. Many common household products—including cleaners, candles, and personal care items—contain chemicals that can act as endocrine disruptors, meaning they may interfere with the body's normal hormonal signaling and contribute to physiological stress and inflammation over time. Research published in *Environmental Health Perspectives* has documented the presence of these hormone-disrupting chemicals in everyday consumer products, often in combinations not fully disclosed on product labels (Dodson et al., 2012).

Reducing exposure by choosing products with fewer synthetic ingredients—such as plant-based cleaners, fragrance-free or low-toxicity candles, and simpler personal care formulations—can help lower overall chemical burden and support a healthier internal environment. Many people report improvements in comfort, energy, and mental clarity when they reduce daily exposure to irritating or chemically complex products, creating a cleaner foundation for wellbeing.

Next, invite life into your space. Open windows daily to refresh the air and let sunlight flood in, syncing your body's circadian rhythm. Add plants to purify the air and bring grounding, vibrant energy indoors. Small touches, like fresh flowers on a table or a cozy reading nook, shift the vibration of your entire home.

> *"When your actions align with your body's needs—through rest, nourishment, movement, and recovery—you begin to embody your true essence."*

Finally, establish a nighttime ritual. Dimming lights, turning off screens, and surrounding yourself with softness signals to your body that it's safe to rest. A home that supports rest and restoration becomes a sanctuary not only for your body but for your soul.

Client Story: Elena's Sanctuary Transformation

Elena, a 40-year-old nurse, felt constantly drained. She described coming home from long shifts and feeling "just as exhausted inside my house as I did at work." Her home was cluttered, filled with synthetic candles, and rarely aired out.

(*continued*)

(*continued*)

We began with small steps: decluttering one room at a time, opening windows daily, and replacing harsh cleaners with natural alternatives. She added plants to her living room and switched to softer evening lighting.

Within weeks, Elena noticed a difference. "It feels like my house is breathing again," she said. The biggest shift came when she created a nighttime sanctuary ritual: tea, dim lights, and calming music before bed. Her sleep improved dramatically, and she woke up more energized for her demanding job.

Months later, Elena reflected, "I used to think of my home as just a place to crash. Now, it's my sanctuary—a place that heals me."

Why It Works Your environment influences your nervous system. A cluttered, toxic space keeps the body in subtle stress, while a clean, natural environment signals safety and restoration. By treating your home as a sanctuary, you create an ecosystem that supports healing on every level: physical, emotional, and mental.

"Physical wellbeing is moving from control to connection, from punishment to partnership, from just inhabiting your body to truly loving it."

When you step inside and feel an instant exhale, you'll know—your home is no longer just walls and furniture. It has become your sanctuary.

Optional Exploration: Fostering Your Physical Wellbeing

Sacred Woman: A Guide to Healing the Feminine Body, Mind, and Spirit, Queen Afua. A holistic pathway for women to restore wellness through ancient healing, ritual, and sacred self-care.

Journey to a Non-Toxic Home: The Room-by-Room Guide to a Healthy, Clean, and Happy Home, Sarah UmmYusuf. Teaches how to eliminate toxins from your environment to support physical and energetic wellbeing.

Atomic Habits, James Clear. Reveals how small, consistent habits compound into transformative results for body and mind.

The Vagus Nerve Healing Bible: Master Your Nervous System in Just 10 Minutes a Day, Lara Namaskar. Shows how to calm the nervous system, reduce stress, and restore balance through short daily practices.

Relentless: From Good to Great to Unstoppable, Tim S. Grover. A motivational blueprint for physical and mental mastery through discipline and inner drive.

Finding Ultra (Revised and Updated Edition), Rich Roll. An inspiring story of endurance, transformation, and the power of plant-based performance.

Body-First Healing, Brittany Piper. Focuses on somatic restoration and body awareness as keys to trauma healing and empowerment.

References

Dodson, R. E., Nishioka, M., Standley, L. J., Perovich, L. J., Brody, J. G., & Rudel, R. A. (2016). Endocrine disruptors and asthma-associated chemicals in consumer products. *Environmental Health Perspectives, 120*(7), 935–943. 10.1289/ehp.1104052.

Harvard Medical School. (2018). Yoga for anxiety and depression. https://www.health.harvard.edu/mind-and-mood/yoga-for-anxiety-and-depression.

Koch, S. C., Riege, R. F. F., Tisborn, K., Biondo, J., Martin, L., & Beelmann, A. (2019). Effects of dance movement therapy and dance on health-related psychological outcomes: A meta-analysis update. *Frontiers in Psychology, 10*, 1806. https://doi.org/10.3389/fpsyg.2019.01806.

Mayo Clinic Staff. (2022). Strength training: Get stronger, leaner, healthier. https://www.mayoclinic.org/healthy-lifestyle/fitness/in-depth/strength-training/art-20046670.

Oppezzo, M., & Schwartz, D. L. (2014). Give your ideas some legs: The positive effect of walking on creative thinking. *Journal of Experimental Psychology: Learning, Memory, and Cognition, 40*(4), 1142–1152. https://doi.org/10.1037/a0036577.

Ramseyer Winter, V., Gillen, M. M., Cahill, L., Jones, A., & Ward, M. (2019). Body appreciation, anxiety, and depression among a racially diverse sample of women. *Journal of Health Psychology, 24*(11), 1517–1525. 10.1177/1359105317728575.

Wasylkiw, L., MacKinnon, A. L., & MacLellan, A. M. (2012). Exploring the link between self-compassion and body image in university women. *Body Image, 9*(2), 236–245. https://doi.org/10.1016/j.bodyim.2012.01.007.

6 Social Wellbeing

Tohamina / Freepik

The Sacred Dance of Connection

There comes a moment when you realize relationships are not about completing you; they are about reflecting the love that already lives within you.

I remember the first time I realized how much I needed other people. As a child, I loved being in nature, but what I loved even more was sharing that nature with someone else. Running barefoot in the grass with my siblings, laughing so hard we collapsed under the summer sun. Those moments were pure joy—connection not just to the Earth, but to each other.

And yet, I'll be honest—after being bullied in school and feeling like I never truly fit in, I convinced myself I didn't need anyone. I equated independence with strength. I prided myself on being self-sufficient, and for a long time, I believed I could do life on my own. I built a fortress around my heart, brick by brick, each layer reinforced with quiet determination to survive alone. I told myself that relying on others was risky, that showing neediness or vulnerability would only make me weak.

But loneliness has a way of whispering truths that busyness can't cover up. No amount of work, distraction, or social media connection could fill the ache in my chest. My body knew it. My spirit knew it. What I craved wasn't solitude; it was authentic connection. People who loved me unconditionally, just for being me. People who would see my whole self, the messy, joyful, anxious, radiant me and still choose to stay.

Slowly, I began to open my heart again. I let small moments of vulnerability creep in: a shared laugh with a friend, a tearful conversation late at night, a willingness to ask for help when I truly needed it. Each tiny act of opening felt risky but also electric, like a dormant part of my soul awakening.

For the first time, I began to understand that connection wasn't a weakness. I began to feel the gentle pull of community, the warmth of being seen, the subtle magic of mutual trust. I was learning that my heart could expand without being broken, that I could show up authentically and still be safe. It was a tender, frightening, beautiful lesson;. Opening my heart was not setting myself up to be hurt; it was setting myself up to be truly loved.

And then, just as I was beginning to trust this newfound openness, life tested me. There came a season when betrayal shook me so deeply, I almost retreated to my old ways of isolation.

Someone I trusted—someone I had invited into the sanctuary I was building—chose not to honor that trust. I remember sitting in my home, curled up on the couch, questioning everyone's intentions. My stomach tightened with fear that every hand I reached for might be pulled away, that every smile could mask a hidden knife. I told myself: It's safer to be alone . . . people are so cruel. And for a while, I retreated, rebuilding walls even higher than before, afraid to let anyone in.

But healing is tricky. It has this way of calling us back to the places we're most afraid to return to. Slowly, Spirit reminded me that connection is not weakness. Love is not weakness. Vulnerability is not weakness. These are the things that make us human, the very things that enable us to thrive. Even in the aftermath of betrayal, my heart remembered what it had once felt; the trembling exhilaration of opening, the quiet certainty of being seen. And though the scars remained, I knew that closing off entirely was not an option if I wanted to truly live.

Recovering from Betrayal

Betrayal has a way of cracking open the soul in ways nothing else can. After the trust I had extended was broken, I felt exposed, raw, and unarmored. The emotion wasn't anger or sadness; it was a deep, aching confusion. How could someone I loved, someone I welcomed into my inner world, choose not to honor that trust? I found myself replaying the moments over and over in my mind, searching for a clue, a reason, some explanation that could make sense of the pain.

For a while, I believed the lie that betrayal meant I did something wrong. I told myself, maybe I'm not enough. Maybe I can't be loved fully. Maybe trusting others is a mistake. Those thoughts pressed against me like stones in my chest, heavy and cold. I wanted to retreat entirely, to never risk the tender opening of my heart again. For days, weeks, months, it felt safer to withdraw, to wrap myself in solitude, avoiding the possibility of further hurt.

But healing, I began to realize, is not in hiding. Healing is in allowing yourself to feel the full weight of the pain while still holding onto the possibility of love. Slowly, in moments both small and sacred, I began to reclaim my trust—not in the person who hurt me, but in myself. I reminded myself that my capacity to love and be loved was not diminished by another's choices. Betrayal didn't define my worth; it defined a choice someone else made, and that is not mine to carry as shame or guilt.

I started with tiny acts of courage. I shared my truth with a friend who had always been steady, someone who held space for me without judgment. I allowed myself to show up in a group when my instinct was to isolate. I reached out for help when pride whispered that I should stay silent. Each small step was a crack in the walls I had rebuilt, and each crack let light seep back into the dark corners of my heart.

"Healing in community happens when you allow yourself to be seen, supported, and celebrated without shrinking or pretending."

Through this process, I discovered that betrayal doesn't have to be a permanent injury. It can be a teacher. It can illuminate boundaries we never set, courage we never claimed, and the kinds of relationships we truly need. I learned to recognize the difference between those who are worth the risk and those who aren't, to honor my own heart as fiercely as I honor the love I give.

Science supports this journey. Research shows that supportive networks and authentic connection not only buffer stress but actually reduce inflammation and strengthen resilience. Our bodies and our hearts are deeply intertwined; when we engage in safe, meaningful relationships, we heal not just emotionally, but physically. Connection is medicine. Trust is medicine. Presence is medicine.

Through it all, Spirit whispered gently, reminding me that vulnerability is not a mistake. Love is not a risk to be avoided. The very act of opening your heart, again and again, is sacred. Even after betrayal, I realized that closing off entirely would have been the true harm. My heart, after all, was not broken; it was learning to beat with wisdom.

Finding My Tribe

There was also a time when I was surrounded by people but still felt deeply alone. I had friends, acquaintances, even colleagues who checked in now and then, but none of it penetrated the quiet ache inside me for deeper connection. I was always the one giving: holding space, offering advice, cheering others on, showing up with my heart wide open. Yet, I rarely felt that same care reciprocated. The loneliness wasn't about numbers; it was about depth.

I started noticing a pattern: I was performing for connection. I tried to fit the mold of what I thought others wanted from me: laughing when I didn't feel like it, agreeing when I didn't fully resonate, shrinking pieces of myself to be palatable or acceptable. And still, my soul felt nothing. I realized that no matter how much I gave or how hard I tried to blend in, I couldn't manufacture belonging. True connection could not be staged; it could only be felt.

The turning point came when I finally stopped performing. I stopped apologizing for my quirks, my intensity, my love for depth. I began showing up fully as myself—the messy, joyful, imperfect, radiant me. And in that radical act of authenticity, something magical happened: My tribe appeared.

They weren't everyone. They weren't the people who expected me to shrink or conform. They were people who prayed with me, laughed with me, celebrated my wins, held me through tears, and called me higher when I needed guidance. They accepted my heart exactly as it was. In their presence, my soul lit up. I felt seen. I felt known. I felt at home.

> *"Social wellbeing begins when you give yourself permission to release toxic connections and surround yourself with people who honor and respect your light and values."*

This tribe taught me something I had long forgotten: Connection is reciprocal. It's not about taking or giving endlessly; it's about the mutual exchange of love, energy, and trust. They reminded me that I am worthy of care, attention, and joy simply because I exist.

Science echoes this truth. Studies show that authentic social bonds reduce anxiety, improve resilience, and even support cardiovascular and immune system health. When we find people who see us fully and allow us to see them, our brains release oxytocin, the bonding hormone that literally rewires us for safety, trust, and joy.

But more than biology, this was spiritual medicine. Spirit had been guiding me all along, nudging me toward the people who would help me remember my wholeness, who would honor my journey, and who would walk with me without asking me to change who I was at my core.

Finding my tribe wasn't an instant miracle; it was a process of patience, discernment, and courage. It required saying no to those who drained me and yes to those whose presence sparked life. Each choice, each act of discernment, was a sacred affirmation: I am worthy of belonging. I am worthy of love. I am worthy of a community that lifts rather than diminishes me.

And when I allowed myself to fully receive their care, something shifted. My heart, once wary and tentative, began to expand again. Laughter came easier. Tears fell without shame. Conversations flowed without fear. Life became lighter because my soul was no longer carrying the weight of disconnection.

"Trust the divine timing of relationships; some arrive to teach, some to grow with you, and some to guide you back to yourself."

Finding your tribe is not just about having people around; it's about nurturing relationships that reflect your truth and values. It's about the sacred dance of reciprocity, presence, and authentic love. When you stop trying to perform and start showing up as your true self, the right people appear. Your soul recognizes theirs, and together you create a space where belonging is not earned, it simply is.

Recognizing the Power of Connection

For a long time, I thought social wellbeing was about quantity. More friends, more invitations, more likes. But I've learned it's about quality, depth, and authenticity. Connection is the oxygen of the soul.

I remember a day when I was walking through the city, feeling invisible despite being surrounded by people. I had a full calendar, meetings, dates, and yet my heart felt hollow. I realized that I was living in motion but not in presence. True connection had nothing to do with being busy; it had everything to do with being seen.

Connection awakens something ancient in us. It reminds us that we are part of something larger, that our hearts are meant to meet other hearts, and that love, when shared authentically, multiplies.

Research confirms what Spirit has always known: Connection heals. The Harvard Study of Adult Development—an 80+ year longitudinal study—found that the quality of our relationships is the single strongest predictor of health, happiness, and longevity (Waldinger & Schulz, 2010). Not wealth. Not career success. Not fame. Connection.

When we awaken to this truth, we start to notice who nourishes our spirit, and who drains it. We become intentional with our hearts, choosing relationships that sustain and uplift.

Letting Go to Receive

Releasing toxic relationships is never easy. I remember a friendship that had become a constant drain on my energy. Every interaction left me questioning myself, feeling misunderstood, and replaying old insecurities. I had to give myself permission to step away, even when guilt and fear whispered otherwise.

Giving yourself permission is revolutionary. It says, "I am worthy of respect. I am worthy of joy. I am worthy of love that does not diminish me." In that permission, doors open to relationships that truly reflect who we are.

Permission isn't just about ending things, it's about communicating your feelings and being okay with letting go. It's about choosing presence, kindness, and reciprocity. I started to notice the friends who cheered my victories, who showed up in silence during hard times, who celebrated me without comparison.

Divine Timing in Relationships

Not every connection is meant to last forever. Some arrive to teach, some to grow with you, and some to guide you back to yourself. Learning to trust the timing of relationships is a spiritual practice in itself.

I remember attracting a mentor and new sacred sister unexpectedly. I didn't see the impact at first, but months later, I realized her firm guidance had shifted my perspective and helped me navigate a challenging season. Timing matters. Spirit orchestrates the people in our lives in ways that often exceed our understanding.

Oxytocin, the bonding hormone, shows us scientifically that trust in relationships strengthens our emotional resilience, creating an internal environment where love and support can flourish.

Practice: Heart-Centered Listening

Authentic connection is cultivated through practice. One simple, powerful ritual is Heart-Centered Listening. I began using it daily with friends and family, and it transformed my interactions.

1. **Find your person:** Choose one person to connect with today: a friend, family member, colleague, or partner.
2. **Set an intention:** Before speaking, silently affirm, "May this conversation be rooted in presence and love."
3. **Practice deep listening:** Ask an open-ended question and just listen. Don't plan your response; your role is to witness.
4. **Reflect back:** When they finish, reflect what you heard: "What I hear you saying is . . . ."
5. **Close with gratitude:** Thank them for sharing and offer one genuine appreciation.

Active listening engages mirror neurons in the brain, helping us feel with others. Empathy grows. Bonds deepen. Hearts open.

Relationships That Sustain You

The turning point in my social wellbeing came with the last three years when I found my tribe—the people who prayed with me, laughed with me, encouraged me, and celebrated my growth. I stopped performing for connection and started showing up fully as myself.

Alignment in relationships isn't about perfection; it's about resonance. It's about energy. When our connections honor our boundaries and values, they become a source of energy, inspiration, and joy rather than depletion.

The Sacred Journey of Social Wellbeing

With social wellbeing, you learn to trust your worth, your voice, and the rhythm of relationships. Some connections teach, some heal, some guide. Every encounter is sacred, every bond a reflection of love already within us.

And when you stop pretending, stop shrinking, and stop hiding, you realize you have never been alone. You have always belonged.

Take a deep breath. Place your hand over your heart. Whisper to yourself, "I am not alone." Because you aren't. Somewhere, someone is praying for connection just like you. Someone is waiting for your story, your laughter, your presence. Reach out today. Love is magnified in connection. One small act of presence, one genuine conversation, one heart-centered connection; it's a sacred dance.

"The most sacred journey of social wellbeing is moving from loneliness to belonging, from people pleasing to authenticity, from surface connections to soul-deep community."

Seven Social Wellbeing Rituals

Social wellbeing is built through intentional connection: how we communicate, set boundaries, navigate conflict, and show up for one another each day. These seven social wellbeing rituals are designed to help you cultivate relationships that are rooted in respect, presence, joy, and reciprocity, so your connections become a source of nourishment rather than depletion.

The Setting Sacred Boundaries Ritual

Healthy boundaries are not just rules we set for others; they are sacred agreements we make with ourselves. They are the invisible shields that keep our energy, peace, and joy intact. They enable us to show up fully in our relationships without losing ourselves. Boundaries are love in action—love for yourself, and love for others—because clarity, honesty, and respect are the foundation for thriving connections.

I'll be honest: For many years, I struggled to set boundaries. I said yes when I wanted to say no. I overextended myself for people who didn't reciprocate, and I avoided difficult conversations for fear of confrontation. At the time, I believed that bending myself to meet others' expectations was a sign of care or loyalty. What I didn't realize was that every compromise chipped away at my energy, my joy, and my sense of self.

"Every time you listen deeply, set a boundary with love, or choose compassion over judgment, you are practicing social wellbeing."

Setting boundaries doesn't mean you are cold, unkind, or selfish. It means you are choosing to honor yourself and your life. It means recognizing that your energy is sacred, and your emotional health deserves protection. When you cultivate boundaries, you're not pushing others away; you're creating a container where authentic connection can flourish.

Research supports this truth. Studies show that individuals who establish clear boundaries report up to 80% higher levels of self-esteem, improved relationships, and lower stress levels (Ng et al., 2020). Boundaries give you permission to say no without guilt, to rest without shame, and to create relationships that are reciprocal, supportive, and life-giving.

This ritual is designed to help you tune into your needs, honor your feelings, and communicate your boundaries with clarity and compassion.

Step 1: Identify Your Needs Take a few moments to reflect. Where in your life do you feel drained, overlooked, or disrespected? Choose three areas where your boundaries may be unclear or constantly challenged; these could be at work, in friendships, with family, or even in romantic relationships. Write them down. Naming these areas is the first act of self-respect.

Step 2: Set Clear Boundaries For each area, define a specific, tangible boundary. This is your personal commitment to honor your time, energy, and emotions. For example:

- **Work:** "I will not answer emails or texts after 6 p.m."
- **Friendship:** "I will step away from conversations that are judgmental or draining."
- **Romantic relationship:** "I need at least one evening a week for self-care and reflection."

Be precise, compassionate, and firm. Boundaries are not punishments; they are guideposts for connection that is nourishing rather than depleting.

Step 3: Communicate with Clarity Choose one boundary and practice expressing it clearly to the relevant person. Use *I* statements to take ownership of your needs and reduce defensiveness:

- "I need time to rest after work, so I won't be available for calls in the evenings."
- "I feel overwhelmed when plans change last minute, so I need advance notice whenever possible."

Remember: Your boundaries are a reflection of self-love, not a test or challenge for others.

Step 4: Reflect and Reinforce After setting your boundary, notice how it feels in your body and your heart. It may feel uncomfortable at first—that's normal. Every time you honor your boundary, you reinforce your worth, your energy, and your capacity for authentic connection.

I remember the first time I told a close friend that I couldn't participate in a weekend event because I needed time to recharge. My heart raced. I feared judgment. But when I spoke my truth, something surprising happened: They not only respected my choice but they also supported me. I realized that boundaries don't push people away; they reveal who truly honors your heart.

Boundaries are a form of empowerment. They teach others how to treat us and remind us of the love we deserve. Each boundary you set, each *no* spoken with intention, is an act of sacred self-care. Your relationships will begin to shift. People who are draining will naturally drift away, and those who are aligned with your truth will step closer.

Daily Practice

1. Choose one small boundary to set today. It could be as simple as turning your phone on silent during meals, saying no to an extra obligation, or asking for space after work.

2. Communicate it clearly and gently.
3. Observe how it feels physically and emotionally. Journal any insights.
4. Celebrate your courage. Each act of boundary setting is an invitation for more authentic connection in your life.

Healthy boundaries are not limitations; they are openings to love, respect, and connection that sustain your wellbeing. They remind you that your energy is sacred, your heart is worthy, and your relationships are meant to uplift, not deplete.

The Effective Communication Ritual

Communication is far more than exchanging words; it's the sacred bridge between hearts. It is the act of inviting another soul into your inner world while holding space for theirs. When done with clarity, compassion, and presence, communication becomes a ritual: a way to deepen connection, honor boundaries, and nurture relationships that sustain rather than drain us.

I'll be honest: For many years, I struggled with communication. I either held my feelings in too tightly, fearing conflict, or I spoke without clarity, letting emotion take the wheel. I remember one particular moment during a work meeting when frustration had built for weeks. My words spilled out emotionally and unfiltered. The Zoom room went quiet. I saw the confusion in their eyes, and in that moment, I realized that communication without intention damages even the strongest environments. So I reeled it back and spoke from my heart instead of my emotions acknowledging intention while expressing impact and I immediately felt the energy shift.

It took time, reflection, and practice to understand that effective communication is a balance of speaking and listening. Speaking your truth with clarity, and listening with your whole presence, transforms ordinary conversations into acts of love.

Science also backs this up: Studies show that effective communication skills can increase relationship satisfaction by up to 50% (Overall et al., 2019). Active listening, empathy, and honest expression aren't just feel-good tools—they rewire the brain to strengthen bonds, reduce conflict, and cultivate trust.

This ritual is designed to help you connect authentically, express your needs, and deepen your relationships through intentional dialogue.

Active Listening Exercise Pair up with a friend, partner, or family member. One person speaks for two minutes about a topic of their choice, while the other listens without interrupting. Focus on their tone, their pauses, and the emotions behind the words. When they finish, reflect back what you heard: "What I hear you saying is . . ." or "It sounds like you feel . . . ." This is not about correcting, advising, or reacting; it's about witnessing.

Expressive Writing Exercise Before speaking difficult truths, try writing them down. Choose someone you want to communicate with more effectively. Express your thoughts honestly, and include the feelings behind them. Then, step into their perspective. How might your words be received? This practice creates clarity and empathy, preparing your heart and mind to speak with love rather than defensiveness. For my clients who don't like writing I always recommend voice recording. It works just as well.

Feedback Loop Exercise Think of a recent conversation where you felt misunderstood or unheard. Reflect: What could you have expressed more clearly? What could you have listened to more deeply? Create a small action plan for your next conversation. Even one thoughtful adjustment strengthens your capacity for connection.

I remember a time when I had a misunderstanding with a close friend. I felt hurt, and my instinct was to retreat, to protect my feelings by saying nothing. Instead, I chose to practice intentional communication. I shared how I felt, using *I* statements to express my perspective, and then I listened—not just to their words, but to the vulnerability beneath them. The conversation didn't just resolve the conflict; it deepened our bond. We left the discussion with laughter, understanding, and a renewed sense of trust.

Effective communication, I realized, is a form of social and spiritual self-care. It enables us to show up fully, honor our own truth, and create relationships that mirror respect and love. When we communicate consciously, our words become prayers, bridges, and invitations into deeper connection.

Daily Practice

1. **Set an intention:** Before each conversation, silently affirm, "May this dialogue be rooted in presence, love, and understanding."

2. **Listen first:** Make listening your priority, noticing emotions, tone, and nonverbal cues.
3. **Speak with clarity:** Use *I* statements, express feelings and needs, and avoid blame.
4. **Reflect:** After the conversation, journal insights: what worked, what challenged you, and how your heart feels.
5. **Celebrate courage:** Each act of authentic communication strengthens your relationships and your sense of self-worth.

> *"When your relationships align with truth, reciprocity, and respect, they stop draining you and start sustaining you."*

Communication is not just about words; it's about presence, empathy, and intention. Every heartfelt conversation, every moment of deep listening, is a ritual in social wellbeing. It reminds us that connection is sacred, love is actionable, and authenticity is the most profound gift we can offer ourselves.

The Conflict Resolution Ritual

Healthy relationships are built not only on love and connection but also on the ability to navigate conflict with intention and care. Research shows that couples and teams who practice structured conflict resolution experience greater trust, empathy, and long-term satisfaction.

Here's a ritual rooted in neuroscience and psychology that fosters understanding, deescalates tension, and strengthens bonds.

Step 1: Pause and Center Before diving into a disagreement, take a few minutes to breathe deeply and calm the nervous system. Paired breathing or simply sitting in silence helps activate the prefrontal cortex, improving emotional regulation.

Step 2: Express Feelings Each person shares their perspective using "I feel . . ." statements, focusing on emotions rather than blame. Affective labeling—putting feelings into words—has been shown to reduce stress and open the door to empathy.

Step 3: Listen and Paraphrase The other person listens fully without interruption, then paraphrases what they heard back to the speaker. This simple act of reflective listening can shift the dynamic, showing the speaker that they are truly understood.

In one session, I guided a client through this exact step with their partner. Hearing their words reflected back and asking "Why was this important to you?" enabled both partners to feel seen and validated. The client later shared that this practice changed the trajectory of their marriage.

Step 4: Reflect and Find Common Ground Invite each person to acknowledge the other's perspective and identify shared values or goals. This reframing helps transform conflict into collaboration and strengthens the relational bond.

Step 5: Commit to Action Finally, agree on specific actions to prevent future conflicts and support one another. Writing down commitments or verbalizing next steps reinforces accountability and trust.

> **Tip:** Practicing this ritual regularly, even outside of conflict, builds empathy, communication skills, and a stronger sense of social wellbeing.

The Diversity and Inclusion Ritual

True inclusion begins with curiosity, openness, and intentional connection. This ritual is designed to help you step outside your usual social circle, engage with someone from a different background, and build empathy through storytelling.

Step 1: Choose Your Partner Spend dedicated time—ideally 30–60 minutes—with someone whose life experiences or background are different from your own. This could be a colleague, neighbor, classmate, or community member. The key is intentionality. Approach the interaction with genuine curiosity and an open mind.

Step 2: Ask a Meaningful Question Ask, "What's a story about your life that shaped who you are?" This invites the other person to reflect on pivotal moments, challenges, triumphs, or cultural experiences that have influenced their identity.

Step 3: Listen Deeply As they share, practice active listening. Put aside your own assumptions, judgments, and responses. Focus fully on understanding their perspective. Nonverbal cues, such as nodding, eye contact, and mirroring their tone, reinforce that you are present and attentive.

Step 4: Reflect and Integrate After the conversation, reflect on what you learned. Consider how their experiences challenge, expand, or enrich your own worldview. Ask yourself, "How does this story deepen my understanding of diversity? What biases or assumptions did I notice in myself? How can I apply this insight in my daily life?"

Why This Works Research demonstrates that meaningful, sustained contact with people from different backgrounds significantly reduces prejudice, increases empathy, and nurtures more inclusive attitudes. A large-scale meta-analysis found that intergroup contact improves emotional understanding and openness by promoting cognitive flexibility and reducing reliance on stereotypes, replacing assumption with authentic human connection (Pettigrew & Tropp, 2006).

> **Tip:** Make this ritual a regular practice. Repeating these conversations over time strengthens your capacity for empathy, deepens social awareness, and contributes to a more inclusive environment—both personally and professionally.

The Joy and Play Ritual

Human connection thrives when we feel truly seen, heard, and valued. Research in social neuroscience shows that acts of genuine attention, generosity, and emotional attunement activate biological systems associated with trust, bonding, and social safety. In particular, the neuropeptide oxytocin plays a key role in promoting prosocial behaviors such as generosity, empathy, and emotional connection, strengthening relationships and enhancing a sense of belonging (Marsh et al., 2020; Zak et al., 2007).

This ritual emphasizes presence, attentiveness, and thoughtful gestures, helping you create deeper, more resilient social bonds.

When we intentionally prioritize play, we open ourselves to spontaneity, creativity, and connection. Play enables us to engage with others authentically, free from judgment or performance. It is a sacred space where relationships can deepen naturally, where humor dissolves tension (Martin, 2007), and where joy becomes a bridge to greater emotional wellbeing.

Schedule Fun Commit to dedicating 30–60 minutes weekly to an activity that is purely for enjoyment. This could be a board game night, dancing, sports, a creative project, or even playful storytelling. The goal is not productivity or achievement; it's delight. Put it on your calendar, treat it as sacred time, and invite friends, family, or community members to join.

Engage Fully During the activity, be fully present. Leave behind distractions, work obligations, and self-judgment. Laugh freely, embrace spontaneity, and participate with openness. When you allow yourself to be genuinely playful, you create a shared experience that strengthens connection, trust, and mutual joy.

Debrief with Gratitude Afterward, take a few moments to reflect. How did this activity make you feel physically, emotionally, and socially? Consider the bonds that were nurtured or strengthened. Share your appreciation with those you engaged with—whether verbally, in a message, or even through a simple gesture of thanks. Recognizing the value of shared joy reinforces connection and encourages repetition.

Client Story

One client, feeling isolated after moving to a new neighborhood, decided to start a monthly board game night with neighbors. Initially, participation was small and tentative, but as the months passed, the gatherings became lively, laughter-filled evenings. Beyond entertainment, the games nurtured trust, collaboration, and emotional support. Neighbors who had barely spoken before began sharing life updates, offering help, and celebrating milestones together. The client later shared that these play sessions not only improved their social network but also enhanced their sense of belonging and emotional resilience.

Tip: Even small, spontaneous moments of play count. Try a five-minute dance break, a joke-sharing session, or playful storytelling during meals. Over time, these micro-moments accumulate, boosting your mood, reinforcing bonds, and cultivating a resilient, joyful social environment.

Play is not frivolous; it is essential. By intentionally creating space for joy and shared laughter, we strengthen relationships, deepen empathy, and invite more light into our lives. Joy becomes a ritual, and connection becomes effortless.

The Gift of Presence Ritual

Human connection thrives when we feel truly seen, heard, and valued. Research in social psychology shows that meaningful contact with people from different backgrounds reduces prejudice and increases empathy, fostering openness and more inclusive attitudes by enhancing perspective taking and emotional understanding (Pettigrew & Tropp, 2006). Neuroscience research also highlights the role of the neuropeptide oxytocin—sometimes called the *social hormone*—in supporting prosocial behaviors such as trust, generosity, and emotional sharing during interpersonal interaction, suggesting that biological processes are deeply intertwined with the quality of social bonds we form (Marsh et al., 2020; Zak et al., 2007).

Step 1: Identify Your Circle Choose three people in your life—friends, family, colleagues, or community members—who could benefit from a moment of presence, support, or appreciation. These don't have to be big gestures; even small acts of attention are powerful.

Step 2: Give Your Full Presence Spend intentional, uninterrupted time with them. Turn off phones, close your laptop, and listen deeply. Ask questions about what's truly important to them, celebrate their wins, or simply sit together in shared silence. Focus on them fully, without distraction or expectation.

Step 3: Offer a Thoughtful Gesture After the interaction, follow up with a small, meaningful action: a handwritten note, a favorite treat, a supportive message, or an offer of help. This reinforces that your attention and care are not fleeting but sustained.

Step 4: Reflect and Journal Take a few minutes afterward to reflect. How did this act of presence affect you? How did the other person respond? Notice shifts in energy, gratitude, or closeness. Journaling helps cement the habit and reinforces your awareness of social impact.

Client Story

One of my clients felt disconnected from her coworkers and unsure how to cultivate meaningful connections. I encouraged her to try the Gift of Presence Ritual. She spent 30 minutes each week intentionally checking in with a different coworker: listening to their stories, asking about their passions, and offering encouragement. Within two months, she noticed her team communicating more openly, collaborating more effectively, and celebrating each other's successes. What started as a simple practice of attentiveness became a foundation for authentic workplace community, trust, and camaraderie.

Tip: Even small moments count. Holding eye contact while a friend speaks, sending a quick note of encouragement, or giving a few undivided minutes of listening can transform ordinary interactions into profound social connection.

The Define Your Tribe Ritual

Connection is not optional; it is essential. Humans thrive when they feel seen, valued, and supported, and decades of research show that strong social relationships are among the most powerful predictors of happiness, resilience, and physical health. A large-scale meta-analysis found that individuals with meaningful social connections have significantly lower risks of stress-related illness, anxiety, burnout, and premature mortality, while social isolation and loneliness are associated with poorer health outcomes comparable to well-established risk factors (Holt-Lunstad et al., 2010). Yet in today's fast-paced, hyperconnected world, relationships often develop by accident rather than design. The Define Your Tribe Ritual empowers you to intentionally curate your social ecosystem so that your core interactions uplift, inspire, and sustain your wellbeing.

Step 1: Identify Your Inner Circle (Three to Five People) Your inner circle is sacred. These are the people you can share anything with—your fears, victories, and dreams. They are your emotional anchors, your safe space.

Action:

1. Reflect quietly: Who in your life consistently shows support, honesty, and love?
2. Select three to five individuals who make you feel seen and heard.
3. Write down their names and note one key quality that makes them indispensable in your life.

> **Tip:** Physical proximity isn't required; what matters is emotional presence.

Step 2: Identify Your Support Network (10–11 People) This network consists of individuals you see monthly or quarterly who inspire, energize, or challenge you to grow. Think mentors, colleagues, friends, or collaborators who expand your perspective.

Action:

1. List 10–11 people whose presence uplifts you.
2. Decide how often you will realistically connect and schedule recurring interactions—lunches, calls, or group projects.

> **Tip:** These relationships are for growth, joy, and accountability; they might not be your deepest confidants, but they sustain your momentum and emotional energy.

Step 3: Identify Your Broader Tribe (Social Circle) Your broader tribe is your extended network; people you connect with via social media, communities, or professional groups. These connections inspire, educate, and remind you that you are part of something bigger.

Action:

1. Curate a list of meaningful communities or individuals you admire.
2. Engage intentionally—comment, message, or participate in events at least a few times a year.

> **Tip:** Focus on quality over quantity; your broader tribe should add inspiration and belonging, not noise.

Step 4: Commit and Ritualize Schedule weekly or biweekly check-ins with your inner circle.

Action:

1. Plan monthly or quarterly interactions with your support network.
2. Dedicate intentional time to engage with your broader tribe throughout the year.

Reflection prompts:

- How does each tier make you feel? Energized? Supported? Seen?
- Are there relationships draining your energy?
- Which connections could use more intentionality or clearer boundaries?

Client Story

After moving to a new city, one client felt isolated and disconnected. She had no intentional social circle. Together, we mapped her inner circle (three people she could share anything with), support network (10–11 friends and colleagues she could see quarterly), and broader tribe (a professional online community). Within months, her social life became intentional: she felt supported, energized, and connected. The structure enabled her to prioritize relationships that mattered and let go of those that drained her energy, giving her a sense of belonging she hadn't experienced in years.

Daily/Weekly Practice

- Touch base weekly with at least one person from each tier.
- Reflect monthly: Are your interactions aligned with your values? Do they lift you or drain you?
- Adjust your tribe intentionally. Relationships are living ecosystems; nurture those that matter.

Belonging is not passive; it is chosen, cultivated, and celebrated. By defining your tribe, you create a foundation of support, trust, and love that sustains your wellbeing and empowers you to show up fully in all areas of life.

Optional Exploration: Cultivating Your Social Wellbeing

Sovereign Love, Dené Logan. Explores how to create conscious, balanced relationships through self-sovereignty and emotional maturity.

The Let Them Theory, Mel Robbins. Encourages freedom in relationships by releasing control and allowing people to show up as they are.

8 Rules of Love, Jay Shetty. Offers timeless principles for building and sustaining healthy, soulful relationships.

How to Love Better, Yung Pueblo. Guides readers toward emotional maturity and deeper connection through inner healing and self-awareness.

Set Boundaries, Find Peace, Nedra Glover Tawwab. Provides practical guidance on setting healthy boundaries for healthier, more fulfilling relationships.

Eight Dates, John Gottman and Julie Gottman. Outlines eight meaningful conversations that strengthen love, trust, and intimacy in relationships.

Soft Landings for Hard Days, Jovian Zayne. A compassionate guide to nurturing community and connection during times of challenge and transition.

References

Holt-Lunstad, J., Smith, T. B., & Layton, J. B. (2010). Social relationships and mortality risk: A meta-analytic review. *PLoS Medicine*, 7(7), e1000316.

Marsh, N., Marsh, A. A., Lee, M. R., & Hurlemann, R. (2020). Oxytocin and the neurobiology of prosocial behavior. *The Neuroscientist*, 27(6), 604–619. https://doi.org/10.1177/1073858420960111.

Martin, R. A. (2007). *The psychology of humor: An integrative approach*. Cambridge, MA: Elsevier Academic Press.

Ng, T. W. H., Sorensen, K. L., & Eby, L. T. (2020). Boundary management, psychological well-being, and relationship quality. *Journal of Behavioral Health*, *9*(3), 145–154. 10.1016/j.jbh.2020.03.004.

Overall, N. C., Girme, E. A., MacDonald, G., & McNulty, J. K. (2019). Communicated responsiveness is a key component of relationship satisfaction. *Journal of Social and Personal Relationships*, *36*(8), 2433–2452. 10.1177/0265407518782134.

Pettigrew, T. F., & Tropp, L. R. (2006). A meta-analytic test of intergroup contact theory. *Journal of Personality and Social Psychology*, *90*(5), 751–783. https://doi.org/10.1037/0022-3514.90.5.751.

Waldinger, R. J., & Schulz. M. (2010). *What makes a good life? Lessons from the longest study on happiness. Harvard Gazette*. https://news.harvard.edu/gazette/story/2010/04/what-makes-a-good-life/.

Zak, P. J., Stanton, A. A., & Ahmadi, S. (2007). Oxytocin increases generosity in humans. *PLoS ONE*, *2*(11), e1128. https://doi.org/10.1371/journal.pone.0001128.

7 Financial Wellbeing

Tohamina / Freepik

The Attitude of Holistic Abundance

There comes a moment when you realize money is not the goal; it is a reflection of the energy, values, and choices you bring into the world.

Money is more than numbers on a screen or pieces of paper in your wallet; it is energy. Just like spiritual energy, it flows, expands, contracts, and responds to intention. When I look back at my own financial journey, I can see how clearly this truth has played out. There was a time when I believed money itself was the goal: I wanted to hit six figures, and I did. The next year, I wasn't just making six figures; I was paying my team six figures. I was moving fast, scaling, and expanding.

But here's the honest truth: While the numbers looked impressive, my inner life didn't always feel abundant. I was making money and spending money, with no real structure, no grounding, and very few rituals in place. I thought wealth was about accumulation, but I hadn't yet learned the deeper truth: Financial wellbeing is about alignment, intention, and flow.

It wasn't until I started creating money rituals—practices rooted in clarity, gratitude, generosity, and conscious choice—that I truly began to feel abundant. That was when money shifted from being something I chased to something that served my highest wellbeing and supported the wellbeing of others.

The path of financial wellbeing is not linear. It is a sacred journey, moving through awakening, permission, healing, trust, practice, alignment, and flow. Along the way, money becomes less about survival or status, and more about service, freedom, and joy.

My intention is to share both my story and timeless truths I've gathered along the way. My hope is that these reflections not only help you cultivate wealth but also guide you to create a relationship with money that feels peaceful, empowering, and deeply aligned with your purpose.

Awakening: Money Is Not the Goal

My first awakening came when I hit that six-figure mark I had once only dreamed of. For a moment, it felt exhilarating; I had "made it." Yet very quickly, I noticed the emptiness. The high faded. Instead of feeling secure and abundant, I felt pressure: to keep growing, to keep paying my team, to keep spending in ways that looked successful from the outside.

That's when I realized: Money itself was never the goal. The goal was what money represented: freedom, impact, safety, and the ability to live in alignment with my values.

Money is a mirror. It reflects back not just how much you've earned, but the energy you carry toward yourself and the world. If you're aligned, money amplifies that alignment. If you're out of balance, money magnifies the imbalance.

This awakening is essential because it shifts the question from "How much can I make?" to "How aligned can I be in the ways I earn, spend, save, and give?"

Reflection questions:

- Have I ever achieved a financial milestone that didn't feel as fulfilling as I expected?
- When I think about money, do I focus on the numbers or the energy and purpose behind them?
- What values do I want my money to reflect?

Permission: Receiving Without Guilt

For years, I struggled with the idea of receiving. Somewhere along the way, I had internalized a belief that abundance was only for certain people, or that wanting more made me greedy.

> *"Financial freedom begins when you give yourself permission to receive abundance without guilt and to manage it without fear."*

Even when the money flowed in, guilt often followed: Who am I to have this much? What if people think I don't deserve it? Shouldn't I be giving it all away?

What I had to learn was that receiving is not selfish; it is part of the natural flow of abundance. Just as a river cannot keep pouring downstream without being replenished, we cannot keep giving without allowing ourselves to receive.

Permission also means managing without fear. For a long time, I avoided looking too closely at my accounts because it made me anxious. But when I gave myself permission to face my finances with courage, I realized the power was always within me.

Reflection questions:

- Do I feel guilty when I receive money, gifts, or abundance?
- Do I avoid looking at my finances because I'm afraid of what I'll see?
- What would giving myself full permission to receive look like?

Healing: Releasing Scarcity Beliefs

"Healing your financial life is not about numbers alone, but about clearing scarcity beliefs, aligning with your worth and reclaiming your power."

When I was younger, I absorbed unspoken lessons about money: that it was hard to earn, that it disappeared quickly, that "people like us" couldn't get ahead. These beliefs became quiet background music in my mind, influencing my choices even when I wasn't aware of them.

Healing required me to pause and ask, "Whose beliefs am I carrying? Are they even mine?"

One of the most healing practices I developed was journaling about money memories. I wrote about opening my first bank account, my first job, the way my parents spoke about money. I noticed patterns of fear, scarcity, or unworthiness and then I gently replaced them with affirmations of truth and abundance.

Healing is ongoing, but every layer you clear creates more space for flow, trust, and peace.

Reflection questions:

- What money beliefs did I inherit from my family or culture?
- Which of these beliefs feel heavy, unhelpful, outdated, or untrue for me now?
- How can I begin replacing them with beliefs that reflect my worth and potential?

Trust: Planting Seeds and Letting Them Grow

At one point in my journey, I worked non-stop, afraid that if I stopped for even a moment, the money would dry up. That fear-driven approach left me exhausted and disconnected from my joy.

Trust changed everything. I began to see money as part of a larger ecosystem. Just like seeds in a garden, not every effort produces an immediate harvest, but over time, the fruits always come.

> *"Trust that the universe provides. Every seed you plant, every skill you share and every act of generosity returns in ways you might not see yet."*

This trust deepened when I started giving generously—whether through mentoring, charity, or supporting my team. I noticed that the more I trusted in flow, the more opportunities, connections, and resources came back in ways I couldn't have planned.

Reflection questions:

- Do I believe abundance is sustainable, or do I fear it will run out?
- Where can I practice more trust in my financial life?
- How have the seeds I planted in the past come back to me in unexpected ways?

Practice: Rituals for Financial Wellbeing

It wasn't until I developed rituals that my financial life began to feel abundant. Before that, I was in reactive mode—make money, spend money, repeat.

> *"Every intentional budget, every mindful investment, every act of giving with an open heart—these are rituals of financial wellbeing."*

- Rituals transforming the chaos into clarity
- Journaling gratitude for every dollar in and out
- Blessing my payments before sending them; my favorite saying when I spend big is BAM (be abundant and multiply)

- Setting aside time each month to review finances with intention, not fear
- Choosing to give regularly, even in small ways, to keep the flow open

These practices turned money into something sacred. No longer just a tool of survival or stress, it became a daily practice of alignment, like meditation or movement.

Reflection questions:

- What small rituals could I create to honor money in my daily life?
- How do I want to feel when I interact with my finances?
- Could budgeting or planning become an act of self-care instead of stress?

Alignment: Money as a Tool for Purpose

"When your financial choices align with your highest purpose and values, money becomes a tool for empowerment, impact, and joy."

One of the greatest shifts in my journey was realizing that money is neutral; it takes on the energy of how you use it. When I spent impulsively, it felt draining. When I invested in alignment—with my business, my health, my team, my community—it felt expansive.

Now, I ask myself before every major decision: "Does this align with my values? Does this bring me closer to my purpose, or distract me from it?"

Alignment ensures that money amplifies what matters most, rather than becoming a source of regret.

Reflection questions:

- Do my current spending habits reflect my values?
- How can I redirect money toward things that bring empowerment, impact, or joy?
- What does aligned wealth look like in my life?

The Sacred Journey: From Fear to Flow

Looking back, I see my financial journey as mental wellbeing. Each stage (awakening, permission, healing, trust, practice, and alignment) prepared me to live in flow.

"The most sacred journey of financial wellbeing is moving from fear to flow, from scarcity to abundance, from chasing money to allowing it to serve your highest self."

Flow means money no longer controls me. It serves me. It supports my highest self, my community, and my purpose. Flow means trusting that when I live in alignment, abundance naturally circulates.

This sacred journey is available to you, too. Wherever you are—whether struggling with scarcity, managing growing wealth, or seeking deeper alignment—you are already on the path. Every small shift toward awareness, intention, and ritual brings you closer to flow.

Reflection questions:

- Where am I on the journey from fear to flow?
- What would financial flow look like for me?
- How can I honor money as a sacred part of my wellbeing?

Financial wellbeing is about harmony, not just numbers. It's about awakening to the truth that money is energy, giving yourself permission to receive without guilt, healing old wounds, trusting the process, creating rituals, aligning with your values, and ultimately, stepping into flow.

When money practices reflect clarity, intention, and respect for your purpose, money becomes more than wealth, it becomes a sacred ally. It empowers you to create freedom, impact, and joy not only for yourself but also for everyone you touch.

And that is true abundance.

Aligning Money with Purpose and Abundance

Money is more than currency; it is energy. Just like spiritual energy, it flows, expands, contracts, and responds to intention. Your financial wellbeing reflects your values, beliefs, and habits, and it directly affects your peace of mind, relationships, and ability to contribute to the world.

Too often, we approach money with fear, scarcity, or guilt. But when we treat money as a tool for alignment and empowerment, we invite abundance into every area of life. This chapter is about cultivating clarity, conscious choices, and financial rituals that support not only wealth but also purpose, freedom, and joy.

Challenging Your Mindset and Beliefs About Money

Financial wellbeing begins with understanding your personal money story. It's not just about how much money you have; it's about how you relate to it, how you use it, and whether your financial choices align with your values, purpose, and long-term goals.

Reflection questions:

- What beliefs about money did I inherit from my family, culture, or society?
- Do I see money as a source of stress, a tool for growth, or something to be used without thought?
- Where do I feel unworthy, fearful, or misaligned with wealth?
- Are my financial choices aligned with what truly matters to me, or am I spending impulsively or on things that don't bring lasting value?

For some, money is scarce, and limiting beliefs like "I don't deserve abundance" or "Money is always hard to come by" create blocks in financial flow. For others, wealth exists but is mismanaged or disconnected from values, spent on things that don't nourish, support, or align with their life purpose. Both scenarios can create stress, dissatisfaction, or a sense of emptiness.

Awareness is the first step. Through journaling, reflection, and intentional mindset work, you can identify these patterns and reframe your relationship with money. The goal is not just accumulation, but alignment;

choose how you earn, spend, save, and give in ways that reflect your values, amplify abundance, and support your life purpose.

Remember: Financial wellbeing is about harmony, not just numbers. When your money practices reflect clarity, intention, and respect for your energy and goals, it becomes a powerful tool for growth, freedom, and meaningful contribution.

Seven Financial Wellbeing Rituals

Financial wellbeing is not just about numbers, it's about the relationship you cultivate with money, choice, and possibility. These seven financial wellbeing rituals are designed to help you move from stress and reactivity into clarity, intention, and empowerment, so your money becomes a conscious tool that supports your long-term wellbeing.

The Intention and Vision Ritual

The Intention and Vision Ritual is designed to help you bring clarity, purpose, and conscious direction to your financial life. It's not about how much money you have; it's about ensuring that every dollar, every decision, and every action aligns with your values, priorities, and long-term goals. By setting intentions and visualizing your ideal financial life, you harness both practical planning and the power of the mind to manifest abundance and balance.

Scientific research shows that visualization and intention setting aren't just feel-good exercises; they physically change the brain. Studies on neuroplasticity indicate that imagining a desired outcome activates many of the same neural pathways as actually performing the action (Decety & Ingvar, 1990). In other words, when you consistently visualize your financial goals, your brain begins to treat them as achievable possibilities, enhancing motivation, focus, and problem-solving ability.

Research in goal-setting psychology demonstrates that individuals who clearly define their goals are more likely to achieve them. Specific, written intentions increase the likelihood of success by creating accountability, clarity, and measurable benchmarks (Locke & Latham, 2002). Applying this to finances means that visualization paired with journaling and reflection transforms abstract desires like "I want to save more" or "I want financial freedom" into actionable, measurable plans.

Step 1: Reflect Quietly Begin by sitting in a calm, uninterrupted space. Close your eyes, take deep breaths, and allow your mind to quiet. Reflect on your financial intentions across three time frames:

- **Monthly:** What financial actions do you want to take this month? Perhaps saving a specific amount, paying down debt, or reviewing subscriptions.
- **Yearly:** What larger financial milestones do you aim to achieve in the next 12 months? This could include a savings goal, investment, or funding a meaningful experience.
- **Five-year vision:** Imagine your ideal financial life in five years. Consider both tangible markers—like home ownership or retirement contributions—and intangible goals, such as freedom, security, or the ability to give generously.

Take note of your emotions during this reflection. Science shows that emotionally charged goals are more likely to be remembered and acted on (McGaugh, 2003). Feeling your vision deeply reinforces motivation and embeds your intentions in your subconscious.

Step 2: Visualize Visualize your financial life as vividly as possible. Imagine how you spend your money, save it, invest it, and use it to support yourself, your loved ones, and your values. Include the sensory details: the relief of paying bills on time, the excitement of funding a dream experience, the joy of giving to others, and the peace of financial stability.

Visualization strengthens neural pathways associated with success, increasing confidence and problem-solving ability. It primes your mind to notice opportunities and make decisions that are aligned with your goals, creating a feedback loop of intentional action and reinforcement.

Step 3: Journal After visualization, write down your intentions and vision:

- Concrete goals with numbers, timelines, and priorities
- Values that guide your financial choices
- Steps you can take immediately to move toward your vision

Journaling transforms abstract intentions into tangible action plans. Research shows that writing down goals increases the likelihood of achieving them by creating accountability and reinforcing commitment.

Step 4: Practice Daily Reinforcement Return to your journal and vision daily. Spend a few minutes reading your intentions, reflecting on progress, and visualizing success. This consistent practice strengthens neural pathways, keeps your goals top of mind, and prevents reactive, impulsive financial decisions.

Whether your income is small or substantial, this ritual works for everyone. Even limited resources can be strategically allocated toward priorities, and abundant wealth can be directed with intention to create meaning, impact, and joy.

Step 5: Reflect and Adjust Periodically review and refine your vision. Celebrate progress, identify challenges, and adjust your actions as needed. Flexibility ensures that your vision evolves with your life, values, and circumstances.

The Intention and Vision Ritual is more than a planning exercise; it's a practice of alignment, self-awareness, and empowerment. By reflecting, visualizing, journaling, and daily reinforcement, you turn financial aspirations into achievable, purpose-driven action. You cultivate not just wealth, but freedom, clarity, and alignment, creating a financial life that supports your fullest potential and deepest values.

The Money Mapping Ritual

The Money Mapping Ritual is designed to give you complete clarity over your financial life. By understanding exactly where your money comes from, where it goes, and how it aligns with your goals and values, you gain control, reduce stress, and create a road map for intentional financial decision-making. This ritual transforms abstract money anxiety into actionable insight, empowering you to make choices that support your life purpose and long-term wellbeing.

Financial stress activates the amygdala; the brain's fear center and increases cortisol levels, which can affect sleep, focus, and overall health (American Psychological Association, 2019). Conversely, awareness and intentional control over finances reduce anxiety, promote executive functioning, and enhance decision-making. A study published in the *Journal of Financial Therapy* found that individuals who actively tracked their spending and understood their financial flows reported lower stress and higher financial confidence (Archuleta et al., 2013).

By mapping your money, you're not just budgeting; you're training your brain to see patterns, recognize opportunities, and consciously direct resources toward what matters most.

Step 1: Gather Your Financial Data Start by collecting all sources of income, recurring expenses, debt payments, savings, investments, and discretionary spending. Include fun money and occasional expenses that might not occur monthly.

- **Income:** Salaries, freelance work, side gigs, dividends, or passive income
- **Essential expenses:** Housing, utilities, groceries, transportation, insurance, and minimum debt payments
- **Discretionary spending:** Dining out, entertainment, hobbies, subscriptions, and travel
- **Savings and giving:** Emergency funds, retirement contributions, charitable giving, and investments

> **Tip:** Use tools like budgeting apps, bank statements, or spreadsheets to get an accurate picture. Seeing every dollar creates transparency and eliminates blind spots.

Step 2: Visualize Your Flows Once all financial data is gathered, create a visual map of your money. You can use columns, charts, or even color-coded diagrams. Then ask yourself these questions:

- Where does money flow effortlessly, like automatic bills or recurring subscriptions?

- Where is it wasted or misaligned, such as impulse purchases or subscriptions you no longer use?
- Where does it create joy, security, or growth?

This visual representation reveals patterns that may not be obvious. Neuroscience research shows that visual learning strengthens memory and pattern recognition, helping your brain identify behaviors that either support or sabotage your goals.

Step 3: Analyze and Reflect Ask yourself these questions:

- Which spending aligns with my values and long-term goals?
- Which expenses are draining energy without meaningful return?
- How can I optimize income, spending, and saving to better serve my life purpose?

Reflecting on these questions creates awareness and helps you move from reactive to proactive financial behavior. Mindful reflection strengthens executive functioning, enabling you to pause before decisions and make choices aligned with your goals.

Step 4: Create Your Intentional Plan Based on your insights, design a financial plan that directs your money toward what truly matters. Include the following:

- **Priorities:** Essentials and obligations that sustain your life
- **Growth:** Savings, investments, education, or skill building
- **Joy and fulfillment:** Experiences or purchases that enhance your wellbeing
- **Giving and contribution:** Charitable donations, gifts, or acts of generosity

Even small income can be mapped intentionally, and even abundant resources benefit from alignment. The plan ensures that money becomes a tool for freedom, growth, and purpose, not a source of stress or misalignment.

Step 5: Review and Adjust Regularly

- **Weekly:** Check flows and spending against your plan. Are you on track? Are there areas that need adjustment?
- **Monthly:** Reflect on achievements, surprises, or lessons. Celebrate wins and refine your plan.
- **Quarterly:** Reassess alignment with life goals and values. Life changes, so should your financial map.

Money mapping helps everyone—from someone budgeting every dollar to someone with abundant yet scattered resources—see where money truly supports their life. The ritual turns finances into a tool of empowerment, helping anyone redirect funds toward growth, joy, and long-term wellbeing.

Tanza had a six-figure income but still felt financially stressed. Using the Money Mapping Ritual, we listed all her income, recurring expenses, discretionary spending, and savings. Visualizing her flows revealed she was spending nearly $800 per month on subscriptions she rarely used and had no clear allocation for investments or giving.

With a clear map in hand, we reallocated funds to savings, investments, and intentional spending aligned with her values. She began to see every dollar as purposeful. Within three months, her anxiety decreased, she created an emergency fund, and she even started a small charitable initiative aligned with her passions. She said, "Seeing the money clearly gave me freedom; I finally know where it's going and that it's working for me, not against me."

Daily/Weekly Practice Summary

- List and categorize all sources of income, expenses, savings, and giving.
- Create a visual representation of your money flows.
- Identify areas of misalignment and opportunity.
- Design a plan that prioritizes values, growth, joy, and contribution.
- Reflect weekly and monthly; adjust as needed.

The Money Mapping Ritual transforms money from an abstract source of stress into a tool for clarity, alignment, and empowerment. By understanding flows, recognizing patterns, and creating intentional plans, anyone, regardless of income level, can gain control, reduce financial stress, and direct resources toward a life that aligns with their purpose and values.

The Financial Design Ritual

Financial wellbeing isn't just about how much you earn; it's about how clearly you understand your income, how intentionally you manage it, and how aligned your financial decisions are with your values and life goals. One of the most powerful tools I use with clients is the Financial Design Ritual, a process that breaks down your income into tangible, actionable increments and helps you make conscious choices about your money, time, and priorities.

Whether you're earning $50,000 or $1 million a year, the principles of financial design remain the same. The ritual creates clarity, reduces stress, and helps you see your money as a tool for living the life you desire.

Step 1: Break Down Your Income Understanding your earnings on multiple levels transforms your relationship with money. Here's how.

Example 1: $150,000 Annual Income

- Annual income: $150,000—This is the total earned in a year before taxes and deductions.
- Monthly income: $12,500—Breaking your income into months helps you budget for recurring expenses like rent, utilities, groceries, and discretionary spending.
- Weekly income: $3,125—Managing smaller, recurring expenses and short-term goals becomes easier with a weekly view.
- Daily income: $625 (based on a five-day workweek)—Seeing your earnings by day helps you make mindful choices about daily spending, work energy, and time management.
- Hourly income: $156 (working four hours a day)—Knowing your hourly rate lets you evaluate the value of your time and informs decisions about work-life balance and productivity.

Example 2: $1 Million Annual Income

- Annual income: $1,000,000—This is your total yearly earnings before taxes and deductions.

- Monthly income: $84,000—This is useful for planning larger expenses, mortgages, investments, or significant purchases.
- Weekly income: $21,000 (five-day workweek)—This knowledge enables better short-term planning and financial goal setting.
- Daily income: $4,200 (8 hours/day)—This knowledge helps manage day-to-day expenses and ensures daily decisions support long-term goals.
- Hourly income: $525—This knowledge highlights the value of your time and informs how you invest your hours in work, rest, and leisure.

Seeing your money in increments transforms it from an abstract concept to actionable energy. You begin to see trade-offs, opportunities, and the value of every hour you spend earning or enjoying your life.

Step 2: Apply Financial Design to Your Life Once you understand your income, the Financial Design Ritual helps you structure your money to support your goals, values, and overall wellbeing.

1. **Set clear goals:** The Financial Design Ritual enables you to map your income to real-life outcomes. Whether you aim to save for retirement, buy a home, start a business, or take a dream vacation, breaking your income into smaller increments helps set realistic timelines and measurable goals.

   Action: Write down three to five major financial goals and assign a monthly or weekly savings target toward each. Seeing the numbers in context makes goals achievable and tangible.
2. **Budget effectively:** Knowing your income at different levels (daily, weekly, monthly, etc.) gives you control over your spending. You can prioritize essentials, allocate for discretionary spending, and leave room for savings without stress.

   Action: Create a simple breakdown:
   - 50% essentials (housing, utilities, groceries)
   - 20% growth (investments, education, skill building)
   - 20% joy (experiences, travel, hobbies)
   - 10% giving (charity, gifts, community)

   Adjust percentages based on personal values and life stage.

3. **Invest wisely:** The Financial Design Ritual informs long-term investment strategies by highlighting available resources and priorities. Knowing how much money flows in daily, weekly, and monthly enables you to allocate funds strategically to grow wealth without sacrificing stability or alignment with your purpose.

   Action: Set aside at least one session per quarter to review investments, savings accounts, or business opportunities. Align every investment with a long-term goal.
4. **Prioritize wellbeing:** The Financial Design Ritual is not about maximizing income at all costs; it's about creating a life where money supports your health, relationships, and joy. Sometimes, that means working fewer hours to have more energy for loved ones, or spending money on experiences that bring fulfillment rather than material accumulation.

   Action: Reflect: "Does how I spend or earn money enhance my life and wellbeing, or does it create stress and misalignment?"

   Make adjustments intentionally.

Step 3: Integrate Ritual and Reflection This is where financial design becomes a ritual, not just a spreadsheet exercise.

- **Weekly check-in:** Review your earnings and spending. Ask, "Are my choices aligned with my goals?"
- **Daily awareness:** Recognize the value of your time and the energy behind every dollar earned or spent.
- **Monthly reflection:** Celebrate wins, note adjustments needed, and visualize the impact of your financial decisions.

I once worked with a client earning $150,000 per year who felt stressed and scattered. Despite a solid income, she never felt financially in control. Together, we applied the Financial Design Ritual: We broke her income into daily, weekly, and monthly increments, and mapped it against her goals.

She realized she was spending freely on nonessential items while underinvesting in her retirement and wellness. Through structured budgeting and intentional allocation (covering essentials, joy, giving, and growth) she regained control. Within six months, she had a clear plan, reduced stress, and even began a side project she had long dreamed of, knowing exactly how her income and time supported her goals.

For a higher-income client earning $1 million, the same ritual revealed that despite financial abundance, time and energy were being wasted on low-value commitments. Breaking down hourly and daily income helped her delegate, prioritize, and invest wisely, aligning her wealth with purpose and life satisfaction.

Both clients, though at vastly different income levels, experienced clarity, control, and empowerment. The Financial Design Ritual is not about how much you earn; it's about how intentionally you design your financial life to support the life you want to live.

Step 4: Make It Your Own The Financial Design Ritual is a living practice. Here's how to embed it into your life:

- **Visualize daily:** Start each day acknowledging the value of your income and time.
- **Journal weekly:** Track spending, saving, giving, and growth. Reflect on alignment with values.
- **Adjust quarterly:** Life changes—so should your financial plan. Reassess goals, priorities, and allocations.
- **Celebrate wins:** Every step forward—paying off debt, hitting savings targets, or investing wisely—is a victory.

Financial wellbeing isn't a number on a paycheck; it's the intentional design of your money, time, and energy. By breaking income into increments, setting clear goals, budgeting with intention, and aligning spending with values, you gain clarity, reduce stress, and cultivate a life of abundance.

Whether you earn $50,000 or $1 million a year, the Financial Design Ritual turns your income into a road map for purposeful living, helping you make choices that nurture freedom, joy, and long-term wellbeing.

The Dissolving Debt Ritual: Taking Control of Your Financial Freedom

Debt can feel overwhelming, but it is not a life sentence. Scientific research shows that financial stress activates the same brain regions as physical pain and increases cortisol levels, affecting health and wellbeing (American Psychological Association, 2019). By approaching debt with intention, clarity, and structure, you can dissolve it strategically while cultivating calm, confidence, and control.

Debt is not a reflection of your worth; it's simply an imbalance that can be corrected. This ritual empowers you to face it, track it, and systematically reduce it while reinforcing healthy money habits.

Step 1: Acknowledge and Assess

- **Get clarity:** List all debts—credit cards, loans, lines of credit, and any other obligations. Include balances, interest rates, minimum payments, and due dates.
- **Use a tracking tool:** Download and link an app like Rocket Money. It automatically tracks spending, recurring subscriptions, and monthly cash flow. Seeing the full picture removes anxiety and gives control.

Reflection prompt:

- How does each debt make me feel? Anxiety, guilt, pressure, or frustration?
- Acknowledging feelings without judgment enables me to approach repayment strategically rather than emotionally.

Step 2: Create Your Repayment Strategy There are two main approaches, and you can combine them:

- **Debt avalanche (interest first):** Pay off debts with the highest interest rates first while making minimum payments on others. This reduces overall cost and accelerates repayment.
- **Debt snowball (smallest balances first):** Pay off the smallest debts first to create momentum and psychological wins.

> **Tip:** Consider balance transfers if you have credit cards with high interest. Transferring balances to a lower-interest card can save money and speed up repayment.

Action: Decide which approach aligns with your personality and circumstances. Then, create a clear payment schedule.

Step 3: Budget with Intention

- Using the Rocket Money app or your preferred tracking method, review monthly income and spending.
- Identify nonessential spending that can be temporarily redirected toward debt repayment.
- Prioritize essentials, debt payments, and one small discretionary category to maintain balance.

Mindset reminder: Debt repayment is not deprivation; it's investment in your freedom and peace of mind.

Step 4: Implement Daily Awareness

- Visualize daily. See each payment reducing your debt as a step toward freedom.
- Check Rocket Money daily or weekly to track progress and spending habits.
- Celebrate small wins: paying off a card, saving interest, or sticking to the budget.

> **Tip:** Awareness turns repayment into an empowering ritual, rather than a source of shame.

Step 5: Reflect and Adjust

- At the end of each month, review your progress. How much debt was paid? Did your spending align with your plan?

- Adjust the strategy as needed—maybe increase monthly payments, pause discretionary spending, or transfer another balance to save on interest.

Reflection prompt:

- How do I feel when I see my debt decreasing?
- How is my financial stress changing?

Step 6: Cultivate Abundance Mindset While paying off debt, practice gratitude for what you do have and the steps you're taking. This ritual reduces stress, strengthens resilience, and trains your brain to associate financial action with empowerment rather than scarcity.

- **Daily affirmation:** "I am taking control of my money. Every payment brings me closer to freedom."
- **Monthly celebration:** Treat yourself in a meaningful but inexpensive way for milestones (first card paid off, 25% of total debt gone, etc.).

One of my clients was $20,000 in credit card debt and felt overwhelmed. By using Rocket Money, she gained complete visibility over her spending and recurring charges. We designed a repayment plan using a hybrid approach: The highest-interest cards were targeted first, while she celebrated paying off small balances to maintain motivation.

She also applied balance transfers strategically, saving nearly $1,500 in interest in the first six months. Each week, she tracked her progress and reflected on the emotional shift; anxiety was replaced with empowerment. Within a year, she had fully repaid her debt, established a savings buffer, and had a renewed sense of financial confidence. She told me, "I didn't just get out of debt; I learned how to treat money as a friend instead of a fear."

Daily/Weekly Practice Summary

- Track income, expenses, and debt using a tool like Rocket Money.
- Make intentional payments according to your chosen strategy (avalanche or snowball).

- Reflect weekly on emotional responses, progress, and adjustments.
- Celebrate milestones, even small ones, to reinforce motivation and mindset.
- Practice daily affirmations of empowerment and abundance.

Debt is temporary and manageable when approached with intention, clarity, and consistency. The Dissolving Debt Ritual transforms repayment from stressful obligation into empowering practice, reinforcing control, financial literacy, and long-term abundance. By combining practical tracking, strategic repayment, and mindset work, you can dissolve debt while strengthening the habits, confidence, and resilience that will support your entire financial journey.

The Gratitude and Wealth Ritual

The Gratitude and Wealth Ritual is designed to shift your mindset from scarcity or obligation to appreciation, mindfulness, and abundance. By intentionally focusing on what you have, you rewire your brain to notice opportunities, reduce financial stress, and strengthen your relationship with money. Gratitude is not about ignoring challenges; it's about training your mind to acknowledge the positive alongside the difficult, creating a balanced, empowered approach to finances.

Science shows that gratitude has profound effects on both the mind and body. Research in positive psychology demonstrates that daily gratitude practices increase wellbeing, reduce stress, and enhance decision-making (Emmons & McCullough, 2003). Neuroscientific studies indicate that expressing gratitude activates the prefrontal cortex and ventral striatum—the areas associated with learning, motivation, and reward (Zahn et al., 2009).

Applied to money, gratitude creates a positive feedback loop. Noticing and appreciating financial wins—big or small—boosts dopamine, reinforces mindful spending, and improves financial confidence. People who practice gratitude regularly are more likely to save, invest, and make intentional financial choices, even in the face of limited resources.

Gratitude also combats the brain's natural negativity bias, which makes us focus on what we lack or what could go wrong. By highlighting financial wins, you cultivate resilience and an abundance mindset, opening the door for more opportunities and satisfaction.

Step 1: Daily Gratitude Journaling Each day, take 5–10 minutes to write down three things about your finances you are grateful for. These can range from small, everyday wins to larger milestones:

- Paying a bill on time without stress
- Receiving a paycheck or freelance payment
- Obtaining a new financial opportunity or business connection
- Successfully sticking to your budget
- Having the ability to give to someone else or support a cause you care about

Even if money is tight, you can find something to appreciate. Gratitude isn't about wealth level; it's about mindful recognition.

Step 2: Express Gratitude Aloud Whenever you make a purchase, pay a bill, or receive income, say a short affirmation of gratitude aloud. For example:

- "Thank you for this opportunity to provide for myself and my family."
- "I am grateful for the abundance that flows into my life."
- "I appreciate having this resource to invest in my growth and joy."

Speaking gratitude out loud reinforces the neural pathways associated with appreciation and abundance, making the practice more impactful than silent acknowledgment alone.

Step 3: Reflect on Financial Wins At the end of each week, review your gratitude entries. Reflect on patterns:

- Where do you consistently experience financial abundance or ease?
- Which actions, decisions, or habits create positive financial outcomes?
- How does expressing gratitude shift your mindset or decisions?

This reflection deepens self-awareness and reinforces intentional financial behavior, aligning your choices with long-term goals and values.

Step 4: Integrate into Spending and Saving Gratitude doesn't just improve your mindset; it can influence your financial behavior. People who consciously acknowledge and appreciate resources are more likely to do the following:

- Save and invest for long-term goals.
- Spend intentionally rather than impulsively.
- Give generously and feel satisfied doing so.
- Approach debt reduction or budgeting with empowerment rather than fear.

Even individuals with abundant wealth benefit find that gratitude ensures resources are used purposefully, increasing satisfaction and reducing the emotional emptiness that can accompany excessive spending.

Gratitude is universal and works for everyone. Whether you are mindful of every dollar or have abundant resources, this ritual helps you cultivate a positive, empowered relationship with money. Scarcity-minded individuals notice opportunities and progress, while abundance-rich individuals stay grounded and intentional in how they manage resources.

One of my clients struggled with financial anxiety despite having a stable income. She constantly focused on what she didn't have; her savings felt insufficient, and debt payments loomed. By implementing the Gratitude and Wealth Ritual, she began journaling daily, noting small wins like paying bills on time and receiving paychecks.

Within a few weeks, she reported a noticeable shift: She felt calmer, made more intentional spending decisions, and even started contributing to a small charitable fund. Expressing gratitude aloud during purchases helped her feel ownership and alignment with her financial choices. Over six months, her stress decreased, her savings grew, and she described her finances as "less of a burden and more of a tool for creating the life I want."

Daily/Weekly Practice Summary

- Journal three financial things you are grateful for each day.
- Speak gratitude aloud during income, spending, or bill payments.
- Review weekly entries to notice patterns and insights.

- Adjust spending, saving, and giving based on mindful reflection.
- Celebrate wins, both big and small, to reinforce abundance consciousness.

The Gratitude and Wealth Ritual transforms financial management from a source of stress into a practice of mindfulness, empowerment, and abundance. By consistently acknowledging wins, reflecting on patterns, and speaking appreciation, you strengthen your relationship with money, cultivate satisfaction, and invite more opportunities for growth and joy; regardless of your financial level.

Daily/weekly practice tips:

- Schedule time weekly or monthly for at least one ritual.
- Reflect monthly. Are your choices aligned with your values, joy, and goals?
- Adjust as needed. Financial wellbeing is a living, evolving practice.

Financial wellbeing is not about wealth alone; it's about alignment, intention, and purpose. By practicing these rituals, anyone can cultivate abundance, clarity, and freedom, creating a financial life that supports their fullest potential.

The Generosity Flow Ritual

Generosity is one of the most powerful activators of abundance. When we give, we affirm that life is not scarce but overflowing, that we trust there is more than enough to share. This ritual is designed to connect the energy of abundance with the act of contribution so that wealth, purpose, and joy flow through you and ripple outward into the world. By engaging in conscious giving—whether through money, time, energy, or wisdom—you create a dynamic cycle of receiving and sharing that nourishes both you and the collective.

Generosity is not defined by quantity but by intention. You may dedicate 10% of your income to charity, or you may offer one hour of your week to mentor someone who is just beginning their journey. You may surprise a friend with a thoughtful gesture, or simply hold space for a loved one who needs a compassionate ear. What matters most is that the giving comes from the heart, without attachment, and with the belief that you are part of a larger flow of resources, kindness, and opportunities.

When practiced consistently, generosity transforms how you relate to wealth and purpose. It reminds you that money, time, and energy are not stagnant possessions but currents that are meant to move, circulate, and uplift. As you give, you open channels for new forms of support to find their way back to you.

Step 1: Set an Intention for Generosity Begin by clarifying what you want your giving to represent. Is it a way to honor the abundance you already have? A way to heal old beliefs about scarcity? Or a way to create a legacy of impact in your community? By grounding your giving in intention, the act itself becomes sacred.

Step 2: Choose Your Form of Contribution Contribution can take many shapes:

- **Financial:** Donating to a cause, supporting a grassroots project, or offering scholarships
- **Time:** Volunteering, mentoring, or offering practical help to someone who needs it
- **Energy:** Sending prayers, blessings, or healing thoughts to someone who is struggling
- **Gifts and skills:** Sharing knowledge, creating something meaningful for others, or providing resources from your unique talents

Select the form that feels most aligned with your current season of life. Remember, you don't need to give in every form at once—sometimes, the most powerful gift is the one that feels effortless and joyful for you.

Step 3: Create a Ritual for the Act of Giving Treat your act of generosity with reverence. Before donating, pause to hold the money in your hands, bless it, and imagine it multiplying in the lives it touches. Before volunteering, take a deep breath and silently affirm: "May my presence be of service today." Before offering your time or wisdom, center yourself and remind your heart that giving is an act of love.

Step 4: Reflect on the Flow After giving, spend a few minutes journaling or meditating on the impact. How did the act make you feel? What energy shifted within you? Did you sense joy, expansion, or a softening of the heart? Reflection is essential because it strengthens the neural and energetic pathways of abundance, helping you associate giving with fulfillment rather than depletion.

Generosity is not reserved for those who have excess; it is accessible to everyone. A single kind word, a smile, or a small gesture of support can hold the same power as a large financial gift when offered with sincerity. The purpose of this ritual is not comparison, but connection. For those with vast wealth, intentional giving ensures alignment with deeper purpose rather than accumulation for its own sake. For those with limited means, even the smallest contribution sends a message to the universe: I am abundant, and I have something to give.

Expanding Wealth Energy Through Flow Generosity activates what spiritual traditions and modern psychology alike recognize as the flow state of abundance. When we cling tightly to resources out of fear of loss, we block circulation. But when we release, trust, and contribute, we join the natural rhythm of giving and receiving. This flow creates momentum, not just financially, but emotionally, spiritually, and socially.

As you live this ritual, you may notice synchronicities: unexpected opportunities, new connections, or resources showing up in surprising ways. These are not coincidences but reminders that the universe mirrors back the energy you emit. When you give, you signal that you are ready to participate in a larger ecosystem of shared prosperity.

At the end of each week or month, pause to revisit your acts of generosity. Express gratitude not only for what you gave, but for the capacity to give. Whisper to yourself, "I am part of an infinite flow. As I give, I receive. As I receive, I give. I am a channel of abundance, joy, and love."

Over time, the Generosity Flow Ritual becomes more than a practice; it becomes a way of life. Each act of giving expands your sense of purpose, opens your heart, and strengthens your faith in the ever-abundant nature of existence.

The Wealth Protection and Resilience Ritual

Financial wellbeing is not only about creating and expanding wealth; it's also about protecting it. This ritual ensures that the resources you've built are resilient against uncertainty, emergencies, and unexpected changes. Protection doesn't come from fear, but from wisdom and foresight. It creates a safety net that allows abundance to flow more freely, because you know that no matter what happens, you are supported.

Without resilience, financial progress can be fragile. Emergencies, economic downturns, or health challenges can undo years of effort. But with intentional preparation—through savings, insurance, risk management, and resilience practices—you build a foundation of stability. This foundation supports growth, generosity, and joy without fear of collapse.

Step 1: Build Your Safety Net Begin by creating or strengthening your emergency fund. This is the core of financial resilience. Aim to set aside three to six months' worth of essential living expenses in an easily accessible savings account.

- If you're just starting, even setting aside \$20 to \$50 per week builds momentum.
- If you're established, refine your fund by reviewing your current lifestyle and adjusting the amount accordingly.

This step provides emotional relief. Research shows that having an emergency cushion significantly reduces financial stress and improves decision-making under pressure (Lusardi & Mitchell, 2014).

Step 2: Review Your Shields Protection includes more than savings; it's about reviewing your financial shields. These may include the following:

- **Insurance:** Health, renter's/home, auto, disability, or life insurance, depending on your needs

- **Legal protection:** Wills, trusts, or power of attorney documents if appropriate
- **Workplace benefits:** Checking retirement contributions, employer-matching opportunities, or wellness programs you may be overlooking

Rather than seeing these as fear-based, view them as acts of love—for yourself, your family, and your future.

Step 3: Practice Risk Awareness, Not Fear Each month, reflect on possible vulnerabilities in your financial life. Ask yourself the following:

- "What would happen if I lost my main income source tomorrow?"
- "Am I prepared if a medical emergency arises?"
- "Are there areas where I'm overspending that weaken my resilience?"

Awareness creates empowerment. Instead of ignoring potential risks or becoming paralyzed by them, you gain clarity on where to strengthen your foundation.

Step 4: Resilience Ritual in Action Turn this into a living ritual by setting aside a specific day each month for a resilience review.

- Light a candle or play calming music to create a grounded atmosphere.
- Review your safety net savings, insurance, and risk factors.
- Celebrate any progress—no matter how small.
- Journal about how financial resilience makes you feel. Does it create peace, strength, or freedom?

This transforms what many see as a dry financial chore into a sacred act of self-care.

Step 5: Expand Beyond Money Financial resilience is deeply connected to overall resilience. Consider the following:

- **Skills:** Building financial literacy, negotiation skills, or a side hustle
- **Health:** Investing in physical and emotional wellbeing to prevent crises that drain money
- **Community:** Cultivating supportive relationships and networks that provide resources beyond money

This holistic view ensures you're protected not just financially but also in spirit, body, and mind.

At the end of each session, ground yourself with a resilience mantra. For example: "I am safe. I am supported. I create stability that allows abundance to grow freely."

Optional Exploration: Owning Your Financial Wellbeing

The Diary of a CEO: The 33 Laws of Business and Life, Steven Bartlett. Distills universal lessons on success, leadership, and personal mastery from the creator of *Diary of a CEO.*

Get Good with Money, Tiffany Aliche. Breaks down the fundamentals of budgeting, saving, and building financial confidence step-by-step.

The Automatic Millionaire, David Bach. Teaches how to automate financial habits for long-term wealth and security.

We Should All Be Millionaires, Rachel Rodgers. Empowers women to build wealth unapologetically through mindset, strategy, and financial freedom.

The Psychology of Money, Morgan Housel. Explores the emotional and behavioral side of finance, showing how mindset influences wealth more than math.

High Performance Habits, Brendon Burchard. Reveals six key habits shared by the world's most successful, fulfilled individuals.

The 5 Types of Wealth, Sahil Bloom. Redefines prosperity by balancing financial, social, time, physical, and spiritual wealth.

References

American Psychological Association. (2019). *Stress in America: Stress and current events*. American Psychological Association.

Archuleta, K. L., Grable, J. E., & Britt, A. J. (2013). Financial and relationship satisfaction as a function of perceived financial stress. *Journal of Financial Therapy*, *4*(1), 1–16. 10.4148/1944-9771.1083.

Decety, J., & Ingvar, D. H. (1990). Brain structures participating in mental simulation of motor behavior: A neuropsychological interpretation. *Acta Psychologica*, *73*(1), 13–34. 10.1016/0001-6918(90)90056-l.

Emmons, R. A., & McCullough, M. E. (2003). Counting blessings versus burdens: An experimental investigation of gratitude and subjective well-being in daily life. *Journal of Personality and Social Psychology*, *84*(2), 377–389. 10.1037/0022-3514.84.2.377.

Locke, E. A., & Latham, G. P. (2002). Building a practically useful theory of goal setting and task motivation: A 35-year odyssey. *American Psychologist*, *57*(9), 705–717. 10.1037/0003-066X.57.9.705.

Lusardi, A., & Mitchell, O. S. (2014). The economic importance of financial literacy: Theory and evidence. *Journal of Economic Literature*, *52*, 5–44. 10.1257/jel.52.1.5.

McGaugh, J. L. (2003). *Memory and emotion: The making of lasting memories*. Columbia University Press.

McGrath, L. M., Peterson, R. L., & Pennington, B. F. (2020). The multiple deficit model: Progress, problems, and prospects. *Scientific Studies of Reading*, *24*(1), 7–13. 10.1080/10888438.2019.1706180.

Zahn, R., Moll, J., Paiva, M., Garrido, G., Krueger, F., Huey, E. D., & Grafman, J. (2009). The neural basis of human social values: Evidence from functional MRI. *Cerebral Cortex*, *19*(2), 276–283. 10.1093/cercor/bhn080.

8 The Art of Surrender

Tohamina / Freepik

How Good Can It Get?

> *Emotional freedom comes when you stop resisting what you feel and start trusting that even your hardest emotions are leading you toward wholeness.*

There comes a moment in every soul's journey when control no longer works, when no amount of planning, pushing, or perfecting can open the next door. That's when life invites us into the art of surrender.

Surrender is not giving up; it's giving *over*, releasing the illusion that we must know the timing, the how, or the outcome in order to trust. It's choosing faith over fear, alignment over anxiety, and flow over force.

True surrender is saying, "Even if I can't see the full picture, I trust that every detour, delay, and disappointment is a divine redirection."

It's understanding that every challenge, heartbreak, and unexpected twist is not happening to you but for you, shaping you into your highest and most radiant self.

When we surrender, we create space for grace. We stop gripping what's leaving and start receiving what's meant for us.

How Good Can It Get?

When I turned 40, I was at the height of my career. I had a thriving business, a team of 21, and the lifestyle of my dreams. My apartment overlooked the ocean in Marina del Rey, California, where I'd watch kayaks glide by each morning as I sipped tea on my balcony. From the outside, it looked like I was living the dream.

But inside, I felt a quiet ache. A whisper that no amount of success could drown out. Even in the midst of expansion, something in me was unfulfilled. I had climbed the mountain of achievement only to realize I was hungry for a different kind of nourishment: deeper joy, true connection, and alignment with my soul's calling.

I stood at a crossroads. I could stay in the comfort of what I had built, or I could take a leap into the unknown.

Meditation and the Question

Before making any major decision, I turned inward. One morning, I sat in meditation, grounding my breath and opening my heart.

I whispered a question to the universe, to God, to my higher self: "God, how good can it get?"

With that question held gently in my mind, I allowed myself to sink into stillness. And then, a vision appeared.

I saw the home I would love: peaceful, full of light, surrounded by nature. I saw a partner who wasn't just beside me but truly with me—someone I could travel the world with, dream with, and build a life with.

As the vision expanded, joy surged through every cell of my body, filling me with a deep knowing: abundance isn't just about achievement; it's about alignment, love, and living the life I'm meant to live.

That question, asked first, became my guide. It wasn't just a prayer; it became a mantra. A best friend through challenges, shadows, and breakthroughs. Each time I returned to it, I found clarity, courage, and a glimpse of what was possible when I allowed myself to envision my highest life.

The Move to Atlanta and the Descent

When I moved from Los Angeles to Atlanta, I couldn't have predicted the journey ahead. I thought I was simply moving cities. What I didn't know was that I was stepping into one of the deepest healing seasons of my life.

The years that followed were not easy. I faced betrayal from people I trusted, watched my income dip after years of consistent growth, and confronted shadows I had buried for too long. It felt like I had been stripped of everything familiar: status, financial comfort, and certainty.

Yet in that stripping away, I found something priceless: myself.

Healing is rarely glamorous. It requires courage to face the darkest parts of our story; the grief, the betrayal, the old wounds that resurface when everything else quiets down. Atlanta became my cocoon. It was where I slowed down, shed layers, and learned to sit with the pain long enough for it to transform into wisdom.

Love Manifested

Even as some parts of my life felt like they were unraveling in Atlanta, another area was quietly blossoming: love.

I had carried the vision I saw in meditation: the partner who wasn't just beside me but truly with me. Someone to travel with, to dream with, to build a life of joy, faith, and adventure with. That vision stayed with me like a seed planted deep in my soul.

At first, I didn't know how or when it would bloom. I was still healing, still learning to trust again after betrayal. But I kept practicing my rituals daily. I prayed. I journaled. I whispered to God, "You've shown me what's possible; help me open to receive this next chapter."

And then, he came.

Meeting my husband felt less like a chance encounter and more like soul recognition. There was an ease, a flow, a familiarity—as if my soul already knew his. He wasn't just a partner in romance; he was a partner in purpose. Together, we dreamed bigger, laughed deeper, and loved more fully than I ever imagined possible.

The truth is, love came when I stopped chasing and started aligning. When I let go of needing to control the how and trusted God with the timing. When I focused less on appearances and more on authenticity.

Finding my soulmate reminded me of one of life's greatest lessons: when you align with who you truly are, the right people align with you.

Love became not just something I experienced, but something I practiced daily; through communication, presence, patience, and joy.

We dated for a year and a half and got married November 24, 2024. I'm still in awe.

Loss and Ancestral Strength

And then, my mother transitioned.

I thought losing her would break me completely. For three months, I cried every day and every night. The grief came in waves, sometimes so strong I thought it might take me under.

But instead of shutting it out, I invited her in.

I welcomed her as an ancestor, a guide, a presence beyond the physical. And the more I leaned into that connection, the stronger I felt. Her love didn't end with her body; it expanded, it infused into my being. She reminded me of my strength, resilience, and capacity to rise.

Grief carved me open, but it also revealed a deeper well of power within me. It taught me that even when we lose what feels irreplaceable, life continues to call us forward.

The Seven Areas of Wellbeing

Through this season, I discovered that true wellbeing isn't built on one area of life. Success in business doesn't sustain you if your emotional world is fragile. Financial security can't heal your heart if grief is consuming you. Physical health alone isn't enough if your spirit feels disconnected.

Wellbeing is whole, layered, and interconnected. It's a dance with the seven dimensions that I have laid out in this book: spiritual, emotional, mental, nutritional, physical, social, and financial.

As I healed, I realized each area required rituals, attention, and love. And when one area was nourished, it naturally poured into the others.

Let me share how each of these came alive for me and how they can come alive for you.

Spiritual Wellbeing

In Atlanta, my spiritual practices deepened. Meditation became my lifeline. Prayer turned into conversation. I began to sense God not as a distant figure, but as a presence within and around me.

Spiritual wellbeing is about connection: with Source, with your higher self, with the unseen wisdom that guides you.

My core rituals:

- Morning meditation with the question, "How good can it get?"
- Gratitude journaling to anchor in God's blessings
- Lots of time in nature

For you: Even five minutes of daily stillness can recalibrate your spirit. Ask your own guiding question. Light a candle. Listen for the whisper beneath the noise.

Emotional Wellbeing

Grief, betrayal, and disappointment tested my emotional strength. I learned that emotional wellbeing isn't about avoiding pain; it's about feeling it fully and moving through it with grace.

My core rituals:

- Allowing myself to cry *a lot* without judgment
- Writing letters I never sent, releasing anger and hurt onto the page, along with powerful primal screams and breakthrough breathwork
- Practicing forgiveness—not to excuse others, but to free myself

For you: Notice your emotions without labeling them good or bad. Create space for your feelings to flow. Remember, emotions are energy in motion; they shift when they are acknowledged.

Mental Wellbeing

My mind used to run on overdrive, constantly strategizing, planning, and analyzing. In the descent, I had to retrain my thoughts.

My core rituals:

- Affirmations that shifted me from fear to faith; reframing *all* of my negative thoughts
- Visualization of my future self when doubt crept in
- Protecting my mental energy by limiting news and toxic input

For you: Pay attention to the stories you repeat in your mind. Are they empowering or disempowering? Choose thoughts that align with who you are becoming, not who you fear you might be.

Nutritional Wellbeing

During grief, it was tempting to numb with food. But I found that nourishing my body with vibrant, whole foods gave me strength to face each day.

My core rituals:

- Drinking green juice each morning as a ritual of vitality
- Cooking meals with love and blessing the food before eating
- Choosing foods that lifted my energy rather than weighed me down

For you: Food is more than fuel; it's energy. Choose foods that remind your body it is sacred, alive, and worthy of care.

Physical Wellbeing

Movement became medicine. Yoga, walking in nature, and stretching helped me process emotions that words could not.

My core rituals:

- Daily movement, even if only a walk around the block
- Yoga flows that opened my heart and released grief from my chest; lots of backbends and hip openers
- Rest; giving myself permission to pause, nap, or restore

For you: Your body holds wisdom. Treat it as an ally, not a machine. Move it with love. Rest it with compassion.

Social Wellbeing

I had to rebuild my relationship with my community. Some friendships fell away. Others deepened. I learned that social wellbeing is not about the number of people around you, but the quality of connection you share.

My core rituals:

- Spending time with people who uplifted me rather than drained me
- Being intentional about the energy I allowed in my circle
- Giving as much as I received, creating reciprocity

For you: Audit your relationships. Ask, "Who nourishes my soul? Who diminishes my light?" Choose to cultivate your ideal tribe.

Financial Wellbeing

This was the hardest shift. After years of consistent abundance, my income dropped. But I learned that abundance is not just about numbers; it's about alignment, clarity, and flow.

My core rituals:

- Honoring money as energy, giving it intention and gratitude
- Practicing generosity even when I had less to give
- Aligning my spending with my values

For you: Whether you have much or little, approach money with love. See it as a tool, not a tyrant. Use it to build, to bless, and to align with your highest self.

The Invitation

As I close this book, I invite you to turn the question back to you:

How good can it get?

Not as a wishful thought, but as an invitation to live fully.

To live your best life doesn't mean avoiding pain, betrayal, or loss. It means moving through them with courage, rituals, and trust in your own resilience. It means refusing to let fear, scarcity, or external expectations dictate your choices. It means building a life on your own terms, rooted in alignment, joy, and freedom.

You are the author of your story. Every ritual you practice is a brushstroke, painting the masterpiece of your life. Every choice you make is an act of creation.

When you wake up each morning, you have the chance to ask yourself, "How good can it get today?" And then open yourself to the answer—not with control, but with trust, openness, and joy.

The CHBT Method: Connect, Heal, Build, Thrive

As you step into your next chapter, I want to offer you a framework that has guided me through every season—one that mirrors the rhythm of life itself:

Connect. Heal. Build. Thrive.

It's not a formula. It's a flow; a cycle of remembrance, renewal, and rebirth.

Connect

This is where transformation begins. Connect with your breath, your body, your Source. Connect with your truth and the people who remind you of it. When you connect, you remember that you are already whole.

Ritual: Begin each day with your guiding question, "How good can it get?" and let it orient your energy toward expansion.

Heal

Healing is how you make space for the new. It's releasing what no longer serves and allowing your heart to soften. Feel, cry, forgive, rest. Every release is sacred.

Ritual: Set time each week to journal, breathe, or move emotion through your body. Healing happens when you honor your humanity.

Build

Build from alignment, not ambition. Build rituals, relationships, and structures that reflect your truth. Building is creation in motion.

Ritual: Take one inspired action daily that supports your vision. Let your actions match your prayers.

Thrive

Thriving is the natural outcome of living in alignment. It's the joy that overflows when you trust life completely.

Ritual: Celebrate often. Rest deeply. Give thanks for what already is and what's on the way.

The CHBT Method is cyclical; you'll move through each phase again and again, rising higher each time. Each cycle deepens your connection, expands your healing, strengthens what you build, and amplifies how you thrive.

So as you connect, heal, build, and thrive; keep asking that sacred question.

How Good Can It Get?

May you awaken to your worth.
May you give yourself permission to receive fully and freely.
May you heal every scarcity belief that holds you back.
May you trust the seeds you plant and the flow of abundance in your life.
May you practice with devotion, aligning your actions with your highest values.
May you walk your sacred journey with courage, curiosity, and joy.
And may you never stop asking, with awe and wonder, "How good can it get?"
Because the truth is this: life will keep showing you.

Optional Exploration: How Good Can It?

The Path Made Clear, Oprah Winfrey. A reflection on purpose and clarity, guiding readers toward discovering their life's calling.

Intentional Ambition, Rha Goddess. Encourages aligning ambition with integrity and purpose to create impact-driven success.

Worthy, Jamie Kern Lima. A powerful exploration of self-worth, helping readers release doubt and claim their innate value.

Start with Yourself, Emma Grede. Inspires personal leadership and transformation through authenticity, vision, and resilience.

Claim Your Power, Mastin Kipp. A guide to healing past trauma and stepping into your purpose with courage and alignment.

Rewrite Your Rules, Morgan DeBaun. Challenges limiting beliefs and teaches how to design a life that reflects your highest potential.

One More Day, Niyc Pidgeon. Focuses on resilience and optimism, showing how one positive thought or action can shift everything.

The Ritual of Gratitude

There are no rituals without relationship.

No healing without community.

No becoming without those who hold us, challenge us, and walk beside us; both seen and unseen.

This book is not mine alone—it is a reflection of every teacher, every lesson, every moment that invited me back home to myself.

It was shaped through my own healing journey; through moments of uncertainty, surrender and deep remembering.

Again and again, I was called to return to my body, my breath and my truth.

This work is born from that return.

I honor my ancestors—known and unknown—whose lives, sacrifices and resilience made it possible for me to be here.

Even as I continue to rediscover who my people are, I trust that their wisdom lives within me.

I feel their presence guiding me, protecting me and calling me forward.

This book is an offering to that lineage.

To my family, thank you for being my first mirror.
For the love, the lessons, and the foundation that made this work possible.

Everything I build carries your imprint.

To my community, near and far; those who have practiced with me, breathed with me, trusted me, and allowed me to witness your healing.

This work exists because of you.

Your courage to show up, to feel and to transform is the heartbeat of these pages.

To the mentors, guides and wisdom-keepers—named and unnamed—who have shaped my understanding of the body, the breath, and the spirit, thank you.

Your teachings live on through this work and continue to ripple across generations.

To those who supported this book in quiet and unseen ways—through encouragement, generosity, endorsements, presence, publishing and belief—thank you for holding space for this vision to come to life.

And finally, to you, the reader: thank you for choosing yourself.

For being willing to slow down, to listen inward and to create space for your own wellbeing.

May these rituals support you in remembering who you are, again and again.

May the wisdom of those who came before and the courage of your own heart, guide every breath you take.

With love and devotion,
Koya

Index

C

D